Walsall

Pure nostalgia...

Ah, the joys of starting up a bus on the old starting handle! Or perhaps it was just posed, as the casually positioned cigarette is not quite right for such a strenuous activity. The elder of the gym-slipped schoolgirls looks out of the bus either with interest, with a look of 'who is he trying to impress?', or in this mid-1920s view it just might be her dad who is showing off.

This lovely period scene shows how basic were the buses of the time, with their matchboard-roofed bodies, tram-like windows and a climb into the saloon that almost, by the standards of today, demanded crampons. This Walsall Corporation bus is 20, (DH 1454), a 1919 Dennis-Stevens petrol-electric that had a Christopher Dodson B28F body boasting electric lighting, solid tyres, life rails one could die for, and a lot of fresh air. *D. R. Harvey collection*

Walsall

A nostalgic tour by tram, trolleybus and bus

David Harvey

·ROAD TRANSPORT HERITAGE·
from
The NOSTALGIA Collection

First published in August 1999

British Library Cataloguing in Publication Data

A catalogue record for this book is available from the British Library.

ISBN 1 85794 132 2

Silver Link Publishing Ltd
The Trundle
Ringstead Road
Great Addington
Kettering
Northants NN14 4BW

Tel/Fax: 01536 330588
email: sales@slinkp-p.demon.co.uk

Printed and bound in Great Britain

A Silver Link book
from
The NOSTALGIA *Collection*

Abbreviations

AEC	Associated Equipment Company
BaMMOT	Birmingham & Midland Motor Omnibus Trust
BCT	Birmingham Corporation Tramways *or* Birmingham City Tramways
BET	British Electric Traction
BMMO	Birmingham & Midland Motor Omnibus Company
BTH	British Thomson-Houston
BUT	British United Traction
CBT	City of Birmingham Tramways
ECW	Eastern Coach Works
EEC	English Electric Company
ER&TCW	Electric Railway & Tramway Carriage Works
FEDD	Front Entrance Double Decker
GEC	General Electric Company
MCCW	Metropolitan-Cammell Carriage & Wagon Company
MoWT	Ministry of War Transport
NCB	Northern Coach Builders
NCME	Northern Counties Motor & Engineering Company
SOS	Shire's Own Specification
SST	South Staffordshire Tramways Company
TWM	Travel West Midlands
UEC	United Electric Car Company
WMPTE	West Midlands Passenger Transport Executive

Seating capacity codes

H30/26R	Highbridge, upper saloon capacity 30, lower saloon capacity 26, Rear entrance
UH-/-R	As above, but to Ministry of War specification
H-/-F	As above, but Highbridge, Front entrance
L-/-R	As above, but Lowbridge, Rear entrance
B38F	Single-deck bus, capacity 38, Front entrance
B-R	As above, but Rear entrance

Contents

Acknowledgements

Books that attempt to show how transport in any town has developed over the years are dependent upon someone actually standing in the street and capturing on film that moment, that milli-second of time when the trolleybus went past just as someone was coming out of a shop, or as the driver was taking a last drag on his cigarette before starting off from a long-forgotten terminus. For all the joys of videos and computer discs, it is the camera that still records 'that moment' of social history, and it is to the many photographers who took the photographs in this volume that we are indebted.

When the first electric tramcar went on to the streets of Walsall in 1892, it was still fairly unusual to see anyone taking photographs of moving objects, let alone tramcars. Photography, although over 50 years old, was still a fairly cumbersome affair; huge wooden cameras with brass fittings that used glass-plate negatives, mounted on even larger tripods, were manhandled outside the studio by some fairly intrepid and determined photographers. One can only admire the results, for example the detail in the view of the earliest picture in this volume, of the steam tram in Wednesbury Market Place, taken in about 1889. Even by the time that the last of Walsall's trams were being withdrawn in 1933, there were only a few intrepid enthusiasts who were recording the scene. After about 1950 photography became a more accessible hobby and as a result there were more photographers interested in recording road transport scenes, and in particular the individual vehicles. Therefore to find, select and use photographs that give a representative and yet balanced view of anywhere is dependent upon locating suitable photographs from a wide range of sources.

I would firstly like to thank the most important person, my wife Diana, for her many cups of coffee while this book was compiled.

The search for photographs started in the Local Studies Library, in Essex Street, Walsall, and subsequently searches were made through the Sandwell Libraries archive at Smethwick and the Local Studies section of Birmingham Reference Library. All of these archives were most helpful and are duly acknowledged. A special word of thanks must be extended to the National Tramway Museum for allowing me to trawl through their extensive photographic archive and use photographs from their collection, and especially to Glyn Wilton and Ian Rowson for their assistance.

I would like to particularly thank Alan Broughall, Clarence Carter, Alan Cross, J. H. Meredith, Roy Marshall, Les Mason, Bob Mills, Arnold Richardson, Mike Rooum, Colin Routh, Jim Saunders, Ray Simpson, Robin Symons, the late Derek Williams and to all those unknown photographers who supplied the late Bob Mack with negatives. If anyone has been missed from this formidable list, please accept my sincere apologies.

Stan Letts drew the excellent tram, trolleybus and bus route maps, while Terry Russell and Alan Condie both provided me with splendid scale drawings. Roger Carpenter and Terry Walsh printed some smashing photographs from negatives that were beyond my expertise.

I would also like to thank Richard Weaver for his proof-reading skills and to Tony Hall and Barry Ware who provided a lot of most valuable information, especially concerning the less obvious locations. A special thanks is due to Ian and Kathyrn Stuart of the Waggon & Horses public house, Oldbury – real ale a speciality – for their patience, and to Bill Lacey at the Woolpack, Rothwell, Northamptonshire, and his Ruddles Best Bitter, beautifully kept.

Introduction

Walsall Corporation began operating tramcars on 1 January 1904, buses in May 1915 and trolleybuses on 22 July 1931. Having jointly operated tram services with the South Staffordshire Tramways Company, the dying giant of electric tramway operation in the Black Country, until 1 October 1930, it became the last operator of trams in the area, on 30 September 1933. Walsall's interest in trolleybuses only really took off in the 1950s when the fleet strength went up from 34 vehicles to 61. But this only tells part of the story; the rest of the fascinating history, the vehicles and the routes and services is found in the photographic record of this book.

By the time Walsall Corporation had been taken over by West Midlands PTE on 30 September 1969, the Corporation had something that was quite unique in the area: Walsall was the only operator to be taken over by any of the Passenger Transport Authorities to be still operating trolleybuses, and right up to the last months was an enthusiastic proponent of this idiosyncratic method of transport. Perhaps the same word – 'idiosyncratic' – applies therefore to Walsall Corporation itself. It was a bus fleet that enthusiasts would flock to see as it appeared that for many years the purchasing policy of its General Manager, Ronald Edgley Cox, was to purchase anything that was innovative, new or unusual, always in 'penny numbers', then for the next batch of buses to obtain something totally different.

During his long term at Birchills he ordered a twin-staircase trolleybus equipped for a seated conductor and Pay-As-You-Board facilities, broke the archaic regulations that led to the introduction for the first time in the UK of a 30-foot-long double-decker bus on two, not three, axles,

and at the very end of his tenure finally obtained permission to operated a 36-foot-long two-doored double-decker. Even when standardisation finally arrived in 1964, when the first of 99 production short-length Daimler 'Fleetlines' entered service, only one other operator ever bought similar buses!

Walsall's mechanical and electrical acumen was rather masked by the fleet's diversity. In later years the impression was of a fleet of vehicles, in their contradictory dull-all-over bright blue livery, that was shabby and unloved. What has to be remembered is that the Corporation worked its 275 or so buses extremely hard and over an operating area that latterly stretched from Birmingham in the south, Wolverhampton in the west, Stafford in the north and Lichfield in the east. Well over half of Walsall's operational mileage was outside the County Borough boundary, and as well as normal routes it ran numerous colliery services in and around the Cannock Chase area, which was still a productive area for coal extraction.

Undoubtedly, Walsall Corporation did have its detractors. The hard-pressed fleet usually looked as if it needed a repaint, while the lack of standardisation must have been a considerable headache for the mechanical staff. Yet there was a certain air of expectancy about the town's public transport system, as for a time there was almost something different each month: trolleybus route extensions, old buses with new bodies, new buses with home-made bodies, forays into the second-hand trolleybus market, and chassis types that were almost unique. This was what Walsall had become. But underneath all this was an undertaking that made a profit and co-operated on joint route services with the Corporations of West Bromwich and Wolverhampton, with Midland Red and, from the independent sector, with the Heath Hayes operator Harper Brothers.

This book shows the operating diversity of Walsall Corporation, in terms not only of its vehicles, but also with regard to the local history and geographical vicissitudes. The volume looks at the Corporation's relationship with other operators, and although it concentrates on the operations within the town, the intensive services within the Black Country and the more outlying areas are not forgotten, although services in and around Walsall receive the greater photographic coverage.

Let us therefore travel back in time to Walsall and the surrounding area as it was, and take a 110-year journey by public transport from as far back as the 1890s.

Route maps

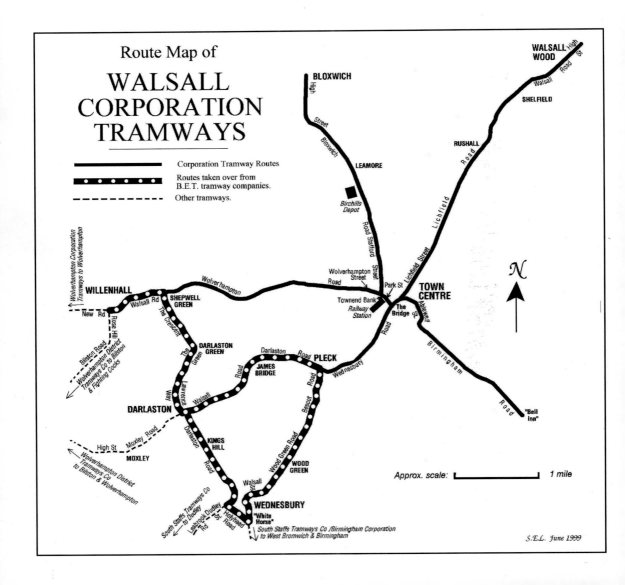

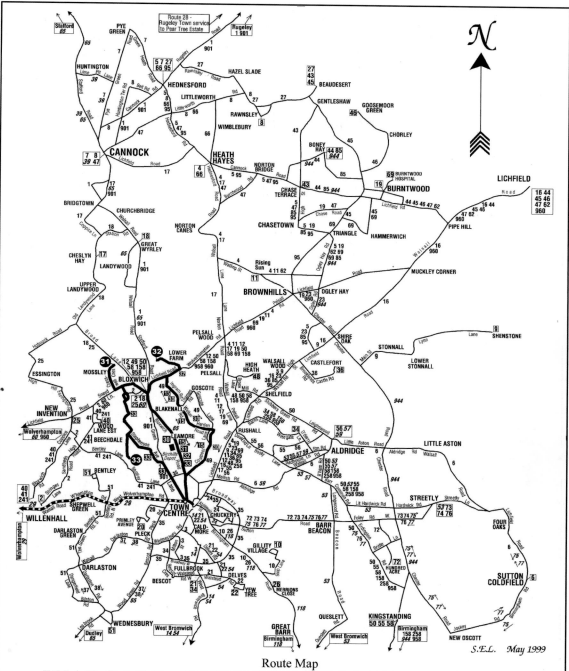

Route Map
WALSALL CORPORATION TRANSPORT

| 2 60 960 | 2 60 | _ _ _ _ _ _ _ Bus route and terminus | 33 | 33 | _ _ _ _ _ Trolleybus route and terminus |

_ _ _ _ _ _ _ _ Bus route, was trolleybus operated until 1965

Network shown is as operated in 1969, prior to takeover of the system by West Midlands Passenger Transport Executive.

Route numbers shown in *italics* denote joint services with other operators:- Midland Red *(39, 65, 75, 77, 118)*;
Harper Bros. *(944)*; West Bromwich Corporation *(14, 53, 54, 57, 59)*; Wolverhampton Corporation *(29, 60)*.

Walsall Town Centre

The Bridge

The historic centre of Walsall was the bridging point of a small tributary of the River Tame, known as Walsall Brook, a river that was first bridged in about 1300 and finally culverted in 1852. It was this river that had given the town its name as it was recorded in 1002 as 'Walesho', which meant 'W(e)alh's hala', or valley. In the same area as the river was the Lord of the Manor's water mill, which was first recorded not long after the settlement was granted a Monday market by the Crown in 1220. A subsequent market charter was given to the town for a Tuesday market in 1417. The significance of this stream is still recorded in the area at the junction of Park Street, Bradford Street and Bridge Street, which is known simply as The Bridge.

The medieval town grew up between the Parish Church of St Matthew on the top of a limestone hill and the fording and later bridging point of the stream at the bottom of High Street. The Walsall Brook separated Digbeth from the newer area across the river in Park Street, and by the 18th century the compact little town, with its already well-established leather industry, began to feel the effects of the Industrial Revolution as coal, iron ore, limestone, sand and clay were all extracted locally. This enabled heavy industry to gain a foothold in the town, which began to expand rapidly.

In 1766 an Act was passed enabling Bridge Street to be built, and by the end of the 19th century Walsall's town centre had moved northwards away from the original market area of Digbeth and High Street and developments had begun along Bradford Street and Park Street. The Victorian market town whose major trade developed around the skills of the leather industry began to give way to the growth of retailing in Park Street and the surrounding streets.

The daily movement of people resulted in the need for an expansion of the town's public transport beyond the London & North Western Railway's route, which terminated in the town's station in Park Street. Electric tram services began in Walsall on 1 January 1893 and the original two routes both passed through The Bridge in the centre of the town. This made it the second overhead electric tram service to be opened in the country, Leeds being first in Britain, opening on 29 October 1891. The two original tram services were taken over from the South Staffordshire Tramways Company by the Corporation, which instigated its own services with its own tramcars on the same date, Friday 1 January 1904.

Above right The South Staffordshire Tramway Company operated two electric tram routes between Wednesbury, The Bridge, Walsall, past the tram depot at Birchills and on to Bloxwich, and from Darlaston, via Pleck to The Bridge and out on the Lichfield Road to the terminus at Mellish Road. These routes were opened on 31 December 1892 using 16 tiny four-wheeled trams, numbered 40-55, which used two 15hp motors to convey their maximum capacity of 40 passengers.

One of the original South Staffordshire trams, 41, displaying an advertisement for Lipton's Teas, loads up at The Bridge in the last few years of the 19th century. The normal female apparel at this time was a long, almost ground-length skirt, but young girls, like the one about to board the tramcar, who today would be termed young teenagers, were allowed to wear short knee-length skirts. Behind the statue of Sister Dora Pattison and the Ionic-columned entrance of the George Hotel, built in 1781, is the open space of Digbeth. Just visible in High Street are the first of the market stalls that lined the street all the way up to St Matthew's Parish Church. *D. R. Harvey collection*

Right Waiting outside Bliss, Ennals drapery shop at The Bridge is South Staffordshire tramcar 30. The tram is working on the Darlaston to Mellish Road service at the new track layout that had been put in place prior to the opening of the Corporation's tram routes on 1 January 1904. This tramcar had been built by Brush earlier in 1903 at a cost of £527 and was one of three of these three-windowed, reversed-staircase, 48-seater open-toppers that ran on Brush's own 'A'-type 6-foot-long truck. It remained in service until about 1920 when it was scrapped.

The tramcar, being a representative of the 'new age', is advertising another recent invention. The original phonograph had been invented by Thomas Alva Edison in

1877, but this used a wax cylinder with a needle moving up and down in a groove; known as the 'hill and dale' method. The flat disc phonograph or gramophone record was first patented in 1887 by Emile Berliner and was to be the method of recording sound that was adopted throughout the world. It used a flat shellac disc and revolved at about 78rpm with the needle moving from side to side in the grooves.

It was in Milan, in April 1902, that Fred Guisberg, the recording 'expert' of the Gramophone Company, persuaded Enrico Caruso to record ten songs for the amazing sum of £100. At this point the wind-up gramophone stopped being a novelty toy and became an essential for every well-to-do Edwardian parlour. Within a few years Caruso's recording of the aria 'Vesti la giubba' from Leoncavallo's opera Pagliacci had become the world's first million-selling record. By late 1903, when this tram was standing at The Bridge, the wind-up gramophone had been adopted by the Edison Company in deference to their original wax system, and is here being advertised on the tramcar's balcony by Mills and Company in Walsall. *Walsall Library*

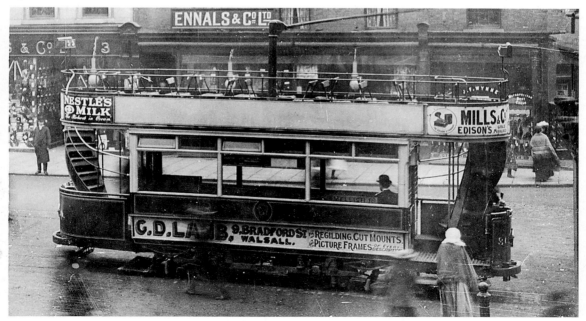

Above   In response to the extra demand, Walsall Corporation introduced its own electric tram system on 1 January 1904. There were five routes and all radiated from this convenient central point, The Bridge. The Corporation purchased 28 open-topped tramcars from the Brush Company of Loughborough.

At 11.00am on an Edwardian morning, Brush open-top tramcar 19, one of the original 48-seaters, waits to depart for Walsall Wood, to the north-east of the town. This was the longest of the original tram routes at just over 3½ miles and involved a long steady climb along Lichfield Road through Rushall. *A. D. Packer*

Below   The 'Patron Saint' of Walsall, Sister Dora Pattison, who was a forceful pioneer in the setting up of Walsall's hospitals, stands on her plinth in front of the George Hotel, overlooking the shuttle of tramcars at The Bridge. Car 9, one of the open-topped Brush-built cars of 1904, waits underneath the large ornamental clock a few years after the introduction of the newfangled Corporation electric tramcar fleet.

The Bridge was the hub of tramcar operation in Walsall and was flanked by the most prestigious premises in the town. To the right of the tram, alongside Sister Dora, was the imposing premises of the London, City & Midland Bank, while behind the tram, in Lower Bridge Street, were the imposing row of shops surmounted by the impressive dome of the Midland Bank on the corner of St Paul's Street.

The woman pushing the large perambulator across Bradford Street towards Ennals emporium is redolent of the age of Edwardian nannies for the children of wealthier parents. On a sobering note, the side-whiskered old gentleman walking towards the camera, if his appearance is to be believed, probably would have been born in the 1840s, which was the first decade of Queen Victoria's long reign! *Commercial postcard*

Right About 25 years later United Electric Company-built top-covered tramcar 30 of 1908, fitted with platform vestibules to give the motorman some protection from the elements, stands at The Bridge. The design of these 3ft 6in gauge trams had a certain affinity to those operated by nearby Birmingham Corporation, which were also supplied by the Preston-based UEC. The importance of The Bridge can be gauged by the number of people either rushing about or waiting for public transport. Even allowing for it being precisely midday, the centre of Walsall was always a busy place. The policeman, wearing his white arm-bands signifying that he is on point duty, suggests that even by about 1930 this tram terminus area was in need of the 'gentle control' of

the constabulary. Coming towards the tramcar, which is loading up with passengers before leaving for Darlaston, is a Dennis 30cwt truck. At the bottom of St Paul's Street is one of the Short Brothers-bodied Dennis Hs of 1928 and 1929, which were numbered in the series 11 to 27. *D. R. Harvey collection*

Below A queue of trams waits at The Bridge at the Park Street end of the tram termini, just after the morning rush hour in the late 1920s. The tram standing next to the clock is Car 40, which was one of ten built in 1919, making it one of the first new trams, for any operator, to be constructed after the end of the Great War. At the time of their delivery, with their open balconies, they looked very similar to tramcars that had entered service throughout the country since about 1907, but, despite having enclosed platform vestibules, within a few years they were as old-fashioned as the steam trams that they themselves had often replaced.

Behind tram 40 is the entrance to Park Street, which even

at this late stage contained turn-of-the-19th-century buildings, although the corner of Park Street and Bradford Street at The Bridge had been redeveloped with a splendidly confused piece of Victoriana, combining a Dutch-gabled roof-line with Art Nouveau detail and large first-floor shop windows, more suited to the Metropolis. Craddocks 'Wonderful Shoes' shared the premises with, among others, Dunns gentlemen's outfitters and a tobacconists. Chauvinism was alive and well in the 1920s.

On the right, adjacent to Lloyds Bank, are two trams working on the Walsall Wood service. The empty tram, nearest to Car 40, is 31. This was one of the four trams supplied to the Corporation in 1908 with top-covers and vestibules, extremely 'up to date' for a narrow-gauge double-decker tramcar. Behind it is Car 4 of 1903, originally an open-topper, but fitted with a short top-cover when about a year old. There was no canopy over the open balcony on this 'Bellamy' top, named after Liverpool Corporation's General Manager who introduced the design. *Commercial postcard*

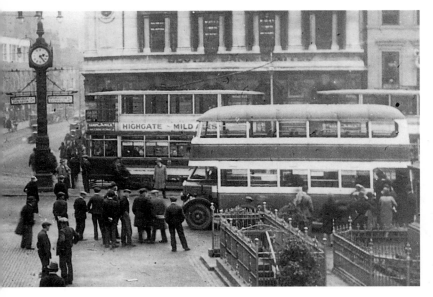

Above Walsall Corporation tramcar 40, working on the Bloxwich service, waits at The Bridge in company with a South Staffordshire tram and the inevitable policeman on point duty; although apparently behind the tram, he is in fact standing opposite Park Street.

Tram 36, alongside, was built by Brush for use in the Birmingham area and, in its original open-top condition, was known as an 'Aston' car. It had originally been City of Birmingham Tramways 219, but reverted to the South Staffordshire Company when CBT ceased operation on 30 June 1911, and was almost immediately fitted with a top-cover. The semi-enclosed vestibule with the 'V'-shaped extension, which enabled the handbrake to be operated, were referred to as 'temporary' screens and seemed distinctly crude when compared to the vestibule on the much lower Walsall tramcar. Car 36 is working on either the Darlaston or Wednesbury joint service, which would be the last company-operated service in the Black Country when it was closed on 30 September 1930. Behind the Walsall tram is Bradford Street with its smashing row of early-20th-century commercial premises, with its most unusual first-floor balcony walkway. *D. R. Harvey collection*

Left By 1931, the 'age of the electric tramcar', as far as Walsall was concerned, was rapidly coming to a close. After 5 March 1931 the only route left in the town was that to Bloxwich, which was to survive until 30 September 1933. All the other routes had been replaced directly by motorbuses, the latest examples being of the sort standing next to the subterranean toilets on which Sister Dora was reduced to standing! The bus is one of 13 AEC 'Regent' 661s built in 1931 with either Brush or Short H28/22R bodies and used in the recent replacement of the Darlaston and Wednesbury trams. Parked behind the bus and dwarfed by the Lloyds Bank building is one of the 40-49 class of trams, waiting to go to Bloxwich via Leamore and Birchills. It is adorned with an advertisement for the local nectar, Highgate Mild Ale. *D. R. Harvey collection*

Above After the abandonment of the tram services to Wednesbury and Darlaston in 1931, the replacement buses were batches of AEC 'Regent' 661s and Dennis 'Lances', with mainly Brush or Short Brothers bodies. 'Regent' 43 (DH 8516), one of the Short 48-seaters, stands at The Bridge beneath the imposing Lloyds Bank building. Equipped with an outside horn, starting handle and radiator muff, the bus would remain in service until 1944, which was when most of the early 1930s double-deckers were replaced by wartime Guy 'Arabs'. No 43 is working on the 37 service to Wednesbury and is being overtaken by a Derby-registered Humber motor-car. *D. R. Harvey collection*

Below With the Imperial cinema advertising the long-forgotten films *The Samaritans* and *The Streets of New York*, tramcar 42 stands at The Bridge before leaving for Bloxwich in the last year of the Walsall tram system. This tram belonged to the last class of ten, numbered 40-49; bought by Walsall Corporation in 1919 from Brush on Brill 21E trucks, they were destined to have only a 14-year life. The Bloxwich route, about 3 miles long, had the sad distinction of being the last tram route to operate in the Black Country, other than those to Dudley that were inherited and operated by Birmingham Corporation. *M. J. O'Connor*

Below The cloche hat of the purposefully striding young lady, coupled with the homburg of the man on the right of the tram, reflects the fashion style of the early 1930s. After 1931, when only the Bloxwich service was still operating, most of the older tramcars were withdrawn, leaving only the 33-39 class of 1912 and the 40-49 class of 1919 to soldier on. Shuttling through Leamore and Birchills, they were something of an anachronism; despite being well-maintained and as up to date as the antiquated Board of Trade Regulations of the day for a 'narrow gauge' system allowed, they were from another time. Car 39, a UEC vestibuled four-wheel car of 1912, has just arrived at The Bridge on the inevitable Bloxwich service and is waiting outside the Imperial cinema, now showing the 1930 film *Old English* starring George Arliss, an actor who provided many music hall impressionists with a good living. *M. J. O'Connor*

Below left For the first 17 years of the route's operation the Bloxwich trolleybuses came in and out of the town by way of Park Street. They turned left towards St Paul's Street then turned opposite that street, through a tight 180-degree loop in order to reach the loading shelters beneath the statue of Sister Dora. A crowd of passengers consisting of women in 'new-look'-length skirts, men whose trouser bottom widths almost hide their shoes, and young children, ankle-socked and having their hands firmly held as they are dragged to the next position in the queue, all wait patiently. They have practised the art of orderly queuing since the beginning of the war some nine years before when rationing first started. There is no hustle or bustle, just a leisurely wait in the sun. The leading trolleybus, 155 (ADH 1), is a Beadle-bodied Sunbeam MS2 of 1933. It is filling up before leaving via Park Street for Bloxwich. Behind the trolleybus and next to Lloyds Bank is Pattisons cafe, renown for its cakes, which compared favourably to those produced by Kunzles, who were also based in nearby Birmingham. *R. A. Mills*

Above The last electric trams in Walsall departed for Bloxwich on 30 September 1933 and were replaced the next day by trolleybuses. This was the second route, as the first trolleybus service had started on 22 July 1931 when two AEC/EE 663Ts and two Guy BTXs opened the service to Willenhall, later to become a through working with neighbouring Wolverhampton Corporation. For the Bloxwich conversion 15 new vehicles were purchased, all with locally built Sunbeam MS2 chassis and numbered 155-169. The first five were bodied by Beadle, the next five by Short Brothers and the last five by Weymann. No 165 (ADH 11), the first of the Weymann-bodies cars of 1933 and here on the 30 Bloxwich service, waits outside the arc of the new George Hotel, which replaced the splendid old Georgian building in 1935. *R. Marshall*

Around the Town Hall

If neighbouring Birmingham was the 'City of a Thousand And One Trades', then Walsall justified its description as 'The Town of One Hundred And One Trades'. The traditional leather and saddlery industry, which had begun in medieval times, gave the town its economic base, and was followed by a specialised iron industry that eventually diversified from equestrian furniture and into more generalised industrial metalwork. In the late 19th century the electrical accessories and switchgear and heavy engineering industries developed and led to a rapid growth of the population and prosperity of Walsall, culminating in the buildings along Lichfield Street, which were a potent symbol of the civic pride and industrial growth of the town.

Walsall's Civic Centre was based around the junction of Bridge Street and Lichfield Street, which was known as Leicester Square. In the Square is the Black Swan public house, while on the corner is the Doric portico of the Regency Court House. The imposing Edwardian Municipal Buildings lie just beyond the Court House in

Lichfield Street; construction began on 29 October 1904, when HRH Prince Christian of Schleswig-Holstein, who had married Queen Victoria's fourth daughter, Princess Helena, laid the foundation stone. Next to them, in Lichfield Street, was the library, opened in 1906, while tucked away in Darwell Street were the municipal baths.

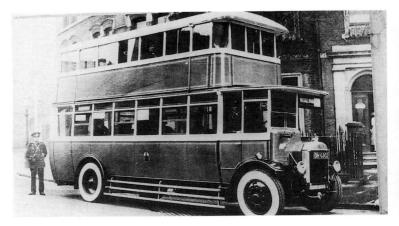

Right In their original state, the Dennis Hs fitted with Short H28/24R bodies must have seemed quite modern. They were equipped with top-deck covers, enclosed staircases, enclosed driver's cabs and pneumatic tyres, which even by 1928 were not all universal equipment on double-deckers. Unfortunately 'le tout ensemble' was built just as some really trail-blazing chassis were being developed by Leyland Motors and AEC. The Dennis E single-decker and this, the equivalent H, were left looking like 'last year's model'!

No 13 (DH 6302) waits in Darwell Street, about to work on the service to Walsall Wood in about 1932. It might look impressive with its white-wall tyres, but a closer inspection reveals the steering column and gear mounted alongside the low-set bonnet. The three lifeguard rails show the true height of the chassis, while the tram-body style of the lower saloon's opening windows was already becoming dated. Within five years the bodies on all the Hs would be reconstructed at great expense to make them look modern, cosmetically at least. The cone clutch and the underpowered, side-valve four-cylinder engine hidden beneath the antiquated radiator gave the game away, and despite the money spent, or perhaps squandered, on them, all the Dennis Hs went for scrap in 1938 when barely 10 years old. *D. R. Harvey collection*

Below Waiting alongside the impressive cupola-topped premises of Midland Bank on the corner of St Paul's Street and Bridge Street in about 1935 are two buses that, although looking modern, in fact belong to different generations. The leading bus is 15 (DH 6304), a Dennis H double-decker of 1928 with a right-hand-gate gearchange and the still common centrally placed throttle pedal. The original Short Brothers body was rebuilt in about 1933 with what effectively was a new one, although apparently using most of the lower deck structure and original fixtures and fittings. It is working on the former tram service along Birmingham Road to The Bell Inn, which by this date was numbered 26. The second bus, 28 (DH 8501), a Brush-bodied 1931 AEC 'Regent' 661, has a much more up-to-date chassis, although still retaining a petrol engine; it is working on the 13 service to Streetly. The 'V'-front of the front upper saloon windows did nothing for its looks, if anything making it look older than the Dennis.

Behind the AEC bus in Park Street opposite the entrance to Darwell Street is a Corporation Dennis E single-decker, while further back up St Paul's Street is the towerless nave of St Paul's Church and a lovely Georgian house on the corner of St Paul's Terrace. *W. Bullock*

Above Tramcars coming in and out of the town from Walsall Wood trundled along Lichfield Street, passing the imposing Baroque-styled Edwardian Town Hall, opened on 27 September 1905, across Leicester Square and into Bridge Street in order to reach the terminus at The Bridge. Bridge Street had been redeveloped in the 1880s, with that confident style of retail buildings that expressed the vibrancy and prosperity of late-Victorian town centre development throughout England. Walsall's town centre rapidly developed as a retail outlet and the shopping development along Bridge Street was impressive, albeit curtailed at its outer end by the five-way junction at the Court House and Black Swan Inn. Flat-canopied and vestibuled former open-top tramcar 17 makes its way out of the busy town centre in the days just before Bridge Street was widened. A time of transition in road transport, there are only three other modes in the street; a horse and cart represents the old ways, while a woman on a push-bike represents the changing social mores of the Edwardian Summer. This would be swept away for ever on the 'playing-fields of the Somme', and in the 'land fit for heroes to live in' came female emancipation and the rise and rise of the motor-car, an early tourer representing the shape of traffic to come! *Commercial postcard*

Right Bridge Street's buildings on the northern side have been left largely unaltered since they were built in the 1880s, while most of those premises on the south side were replaced towards the end of the 1970s. The street remains a shopping street in the town, but it does have a more friendly appeal as the large national and regional stores have not encroached into it. On 21 July 1997 West Midlands Travel Wright B37F-bodied Volvo B6LE 554 (P554 LDA) loads up with passengers, as did the tram, in the middle of the road on the 376A service to Old Oscott. On leaving Bridge Street the bus will turn right and climb St Paul's Street. *D. R. Harvey*

Top Leicester Square is at the junction of Bridge Street (right) and Lichfield Street. To the extreme left are the imposing Doric columns of the Court House, which looks older than it actually is; it was built in 1831 as the home of the Walsall Literary & Philosophical Society. At the junction are late-Victorian commercial and banking buildings looking a little incongruous next to the early-19th-century buildings in Bridge Street. Car 1, one of the six original trams fitted with Milnes-Voss 'white'-pattern 'balloon' totally enclosed top decks, stands outside the Town Hall in a passing loop in about 1912. It is leaving the town centre on the service to Walsall Wood. To the right are the tram tracks of the Birmingham Road service. *Commercial postcard*

Middle A large part of Leicester Square at the junction with Lichfield Street has remained unaltered since the trams stopped running to Walsall Wood on 31 March 1928. The three-storied Victorian Black Swan public house has had a new lease of life, while on the corner of Bridge Street and Lichfield Street the round-ended building occupied by the Cheltenham & Gloucester Building Society has been carefully restored. Next to it in Bridge Street is the County Court building, a far cry from the imposing building on the other side of Leicester Square. No 1513 (P513 KOX), an LPG-powered Alexander-bodied Volvo B10L, enters Bridge Street on the 529 service to Wolverhampton on 29 January 1999. *D. R. Harvey*

Bottom A Midland Red SOS S-type single-decker of about 1924 climbs up Bridge Street as it makes its way out of the town centre following the tram tracks that led towards the Birmingham Road. Most of the early Victorian buildings on the left, including the toilet brush maker, J. Adcock, were swept away in the 1920s by the buildings that have become the Walsall County Court. Two of the town's theatres being advertised here, (both in Park Street) look as if they are going through a bad patch; Her Majesty's is offering a 'Great Novelty Programme' entitled 'Movies In The Making', while at the Grand a twice nightly performance of 'The Operatic Concert Party' is available for the discerning theatre-goer. A third theatre, The Imperial, was in Darwell Street. *Commercial postcard*

Walsall's grandest street was in reality only a small section of Lichfield Street from the Bridge Street junction at Leicester Square. The Court House, the Town Hall and the Library grace the north side of Lichfield Street, while opposite and out of sight were a number of quite attractive Regency town-houses, some surviving today in the menial role of offices.

It is about 1935 and the crossing point around Leicester Square has been fitted with a new pedestrian aid, the Belisha Beacon, named after the Minister of Transport, Mr

Leslie Hore-Belisha, who introduced them. It would not be until 1951 that the road was given black and white stripes and they became known as Zebra Crossings. Going around the traffic island in front of Windridge's pram shop is a speeding unidentifiable AEC 'Regent' 661, which entered service in 1931. It is turning into Bridge Street and could be working on the former 2-mile Birmingham Road tram service that had been abandoned on 30 September 1929. The bus is being followed by an almost new Wolseley Fourteen car. *Walsall Local Studies Library*

The mid-Edwardian Lichfield Street rapidly became the most impressive street in the town. Walsall Corporation open-topped tramcar 17 stands in the passing loop at Leicester Square, opposite the Doric columns of the County Court building. The tram has worked in from Rushall, about half-way along the route to Walsall Wood. The very straight Lichfield Street disappears into the distance at the point where the entrance to the Arboretum is located.

Very soon after the completion of the baroque-towered Town Hall in 1905 and the library beyond Tower Street by 1906, the Corporation tram lines on the Walsall Wood service were doubled along Lichfield Street, although the original South Staffordshire electric line had no passing loops at this point. Within four years of entering service this tram received a canopied top-cover, so that dates this lovely sunny day to about 1907. *National Tramway Museum*

Right Waiting at roughly the same place in the passing loop in Lichfield Street as Car 17, but about 20 years later, is Brush-built tram 10, which has come in from Walsall Wood. The large building behind the tram is the main Walsall Library, opened in 1906 and built with the aid of an endowment of £8,000 from the philanthropist Andrew Carnegie. The tram, originally open-topped but fitted with a top-cover quite early in its life and later vestibuled by 1916, was retrucked with Brill 21E units in 1919. The resulting vehicle retained only its original lower saloon and, despite all these alterations, would be withdrawn by 1931, some three years after this picture was taken. This route was abandoned on 1 April 1928. *D. R. Harvey collection*

Right Having just passed the Town Hall is Leyland 'Titan' PD1 199 (EED 10). Built in 1947, it was purchased in 1959, along with EED 9, from Warrington Corporation, where it had been numbered 101. The two buses had low-bridge 53-seater Bruce bodies and were purchased for the routes where there was insufficient clearance beneath bridges. No 199 is working on one of these services to Aldridge, not long after being purchased; it is passing a Morris Oxford and a Standard 10, both of which are only three or four years old. Even by this date most of the houses along Lichfield Street had been converted to offices, such as that occupied by Gilbert, Son & James. *L. Mason*

Park Street

For most of this century Park Street was open for vehicular traffic, as it linked the town centre at The Bridge with Townend Bank and the main roads out towards Wolverhampton and Bloxwich. It developed in the mid-19th century as a shopping street when Walsall's market was extended from its traditional medieval position in Digbeth and High Street. By the time the trams were introduced on the Bloxwich service on 1 January 1904, the street could boast the two main theatres in the town, The Grand and Her Majesty's as well as the main railway station entrance. It also had three inns and five public houses, such as the Freemasons' Arms, which were the 'other' social centres

in the town. Today only the Red Lion, a Banks's public house, remains, opposite the Quasar Centre, in a magnificent Victorian building dating from 1896.

Park Street also developed as the second area of finance in the town after The Bridge, and still retains this function. For many years the street resisted the trend to copy the larger Birmingham and Wolverhampton shopping centres and retained the comforting feel of a shopping street that was still operating at a human scale. The result is that there are no high-rise buildings in the town centre, and recent rebuilding, as is the case at the bottom of Park Street opposite Lloyds Bank, has been done with brick-faced buildings, rather than the uninspired block of 1950s premises occupied by, among others, the National Westminster Bank and Thorntons.

Although pedestrianised, Park Street remains the most important shopping street in Walsall, having in it shops owned by the large multi-nationals such as Boots the Chemist, Littlewoods, Marks & Spencer, Next, W. H. Smith, Dixons and even McDonalds. At the top end of Park Street some of the older buildings were swept away with the construction of the Quasar Centre. The more recent modern Saddlers Shopping Centre is a fairly well-hidden indoor shopping centre. The Saddlers Centre was built mainly on the site of the old railway goods sheds, and as part of its construction the railway station was also included in the scheme. This reduced the three-times-rebuilt Walsall railway station to a gloomy subterranean 'tunnel', with its main entrance being 'round the corner' in Station Street. The entrances to the Saddlers Centre were more successful with understated entrances in Park Street at the one end and Bradford Place at the other.

Below The removal of the inward journey of the Bloxwich trolleybuses from Park Street into St Paul's Street in September 1950 must have made life considerably easier for their drivers; they must have dreaded the muscle-wrenching turning circle at The Bridge. Trolleybuses in general are renowned for their heavy steering and anyone who could make a 180-degree turn in a pre-war six-wheeled trolleybus look easy has to be admired!

Trolleybus 160 (ADH 6), which weighed 8 tons 8 cwt 3 quarters, displays certain 'Trolleybusesque' features, such as the double waistrail panel on the lower saloon, which was used to store the trolley retrieval pole, and the double-platform step arrangement of these early Sunbeam MS2s, of which 160 was only the 16th to be manufactured. It is about to turn into Park Street from The Bridge in August 1950, just before the service was redirected, having just left the rudimentary shelters in front of the rebuilt George Hotel of 1935. To the left is Lloyds Bank, while behind the trolleybus, through the foliage, is St Paul's Street. *C. Carter*

Below left An unidentified South Staffordshire tramcar, from the original 40-55 batch, comes down Park Street towards The Bridge in about 1894 in the days before the tram tracks were doubled. The very plain, almost modern-looking traction poles span only half the street and carry only a single tram wire. Many of the first generation buildings to be erected in Park Street earlier in the century still remain, including the Three Cups Inn, which would be demolished by the turn of the century.

The Grand Theatre and its tower, opened in 1890, dominates the distant skyline, but the hotchpotch of buildings at Townend Bank, which included Harris's hay and straw chandlers, have yet to be demolished. The imposing Her Majesty's Theatre was not opened until 1900, and its distant ghostly outline is just visible in the next view, taken perhaps ten years later. *D. R. Harvey collection*

Above Car 24, one of the Brush-built 54-seat open-topped trams that entered service on 1 January 1904, has come down Park Street and is approaching the junction at The Bridge, with the still fairly new Lloyds Bank building on the right-hand corner. Of the retail outlets in Park Street, only the Maypole provisions merchant can be readily identified. The Maypole shops, rather like Wrensons, was an important West Midlands grocery retailer, who only succumbed to the major supermarket onslaughts in the late 1960s. The globular light shades hanging outside many of the shops on the left-hand side of Park Street were a typical Edwardian feature and somehow symbolised through the medium of the newfangled electric light the town's prosperity. The distant building with the tower is The Grand Theatre, which would dominate the skyline until the retailing redevelopment swept it away. *D. R. Harvey collection*

Right Unlike many towns that have been subjected to pedestrianisation schemes, much of the original fabric of Park Street remains from the time before the Second World War. The Lloyds Bank building, which appears so prominently in the early tram photographs, still remains, as do some of the shops a little further up the street. Just visible is the round sign that identifies the entrance to the Saddlers Centre, which opened for business on 24 March 1980. This 29 January 1999 view from The Bridge end of Park Street shows that the old entertainment sites have long since disappeared, with even the distant Townend Bank being devoid of a cinema. *D. R. Harvey*

Below The almost new, locally registered Morris 1100 of 1966 dates this view of Park Street as during the 'Swinging Sixties', although whether they were swinging in Walsall is debatable, for the decline of many heavy engineering companies had its roots about this time.

Park Street not only supplied the 'outer' needs of the well-dressed man and woman but, unlike many town centres today, also still had thriving, locally based, grocers and provisions merchants, butchers and greengrocers shops. Marsh & Baxter, for example, were a reputable pork butcher based in Dale End in Birmingham. They had an excellent reputation for their pork pies, pork sausages and bacon as well as local delicacies such as faggots, black pudding, pigs' trotters and chawl, which were more of an acquired taste. It is historically appropriate that they were a pork butcher, for throughout the 19th century Walsall had one of the main pig markets in the country, and Marsh & Baxter's shop provides an interesting link to the days when over 2,000 pigs a day were being slaughtered in the town.

By this time the old family-run shops of the town centre were rapidly being replaced by larger, nationwide outlets. To the right and next to Lloyds Bank is Dorothy Perkins, well-known for its ladies' lingerie, which at the time of writing remains in the same location. Next door, in 1966, is the Saxone shoe shop.

The bus, 812 (RDH 502), is working on the long 65 service from Stafford via Bloxwich to Dudley. Ten of these very stylish-looking Leyland 'Titan' PD2/12 buses entered service in May and June of 1953. Their 58-seater bodies were ordered from Park Royal, but were built by Charles Roe of Crossgates, Leeds. In 1959 and 1960 the first three were lengthened by 3 feet by Willowbrook's of Loughborough, and at the same time were converted to forward entrances and front staircases. This increased their seating capacity by 13 and gave them an FH39/32F layout. All ten remained to be taken over by West Midlands PTE on 1 October 1969, three of the unconverted ones lasting until 1973. *M. Fenton*

Park Street, Walsall

Below left Walsall Brook, a tributary of the River Tame, flows under Park Street and creates sufficient of a valley that the Victorian engineers of the then South Staffordshire Railway used the advantages of the natural topography to construct the railway line from Birmingham. By the time it opened on 1 November 1847 it was being operated by the London & North Western Railway (LNWR). The site at Park Street was the third station to be opened in 1 January 1884, but has always been prone to flooding, despite numerous attempts to put in flood-controlling culverts. The result is that the centre of Walsall has always been a victim of the natural drainage of the area. Even in this, the first decade of the 20th century, parts of the town centre were prone to being flooded quite badly.

Brush open-topped tramcar 24 of 1904 travels up the hill in Park Street towards the slight hump in the road that marks the position of the culverted stream. It is carrying on its balcony panel an advertisement for 'Bovril', a beverage that had begun life in the previous century and is still with us today. The tramcar is on its way to Bloxwich via Townend Bank. *Commercial postcard*

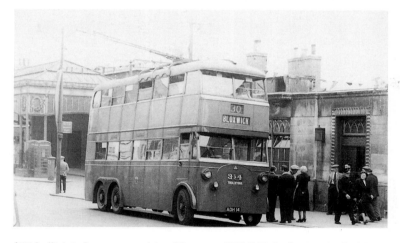

Above Edwardian views of electric tramcars, irrespective of their location, or even how long the service had been in operation, seemed to attract children in the same way that 25 years later everyone went out and pointed to the sky when an aeroplane flew overhead. The electric tram was the wonder of the age and the importance of the tram system to the mobility of the local population in towns like Walsall can be judged by the number of passengers that tramcar 22 is bringing in from Bloxwich and the lack of any other vehicular traffic in Park Street. With trams being limited to no more than 4mph in the town centre, the almost free movement of pedestrians rather echoed the pedestrianised Park Street of 90 years later. The tram is passing the wrought-iron canopy at the entrance of Walsall's jointly operated LNWR and Midland Railway station in about 1908, while on the left the Double Value 6½d Bazaar Arcade is being advertised on a placard. *Commercial postcard*

Above right Almost 50 years later and in almost the same position is trolleybus ADH 14, working on the 30 service to Bloxwich in about 1951. It had originally been numbered 168 in Walsall's fleet, but became 314 in 1950 when it was already 17 years old. As usual for all the post-1933 orders for trolleybuses, this vehicle was a very early Sunbeam MS2 model, which had only been introduced by the Wolverhampton-based manufacturer during the previous year, and was fitted with a composite-construction Weymann H32/28R body. Despite looking a little 'down at heel', the five Weymann-bodied Sunbeams stayed in service until 1955, which was about five years longer than the contemporary five Beadle or five Short-bodied examples.

The Salvation Army Officer strides determinedly past the men waiting outside the licensed premises, whose licensee was one William Platt. These occupied the remnants of the old Grand Theatre, which stood on the corner of Park Street and Station Street. In the background is the rather splendid entrance to the railway booking hall and station, built in 1884 but replaced in 1923 after the original had been destroyed by fire in 1916, only to be swept away altogether in 1978. *J. H. Taylforth collection*

Below Walsall station's 1923 frontage was still intact on 10 April 1965 and looking for all the world as though it would last for a long time. By the turn of the century up to 1,000 LNWR and MR trains passed through the station in 24 hours. After passing into LMS ownership at the Grouping in 1923, then to the Nationalised British Railways in 1948, the railway station went into a period of slow decline, and in 1978 it was demolished to make way for The Saddler's Centre. In this 'Swinging Sixties' look at the railway station in Park Street, with a day trip to Liverpool costing 21 shillings, the central focus was Finlay's kiosk. Advertising a 24-hour service, which probably involved a cigarette machine, the kiosk sold cigarettes, tobacco and confectionery, although the Durham Ox public house next door might have more customers at certain times of the day. *R. J. Essery*

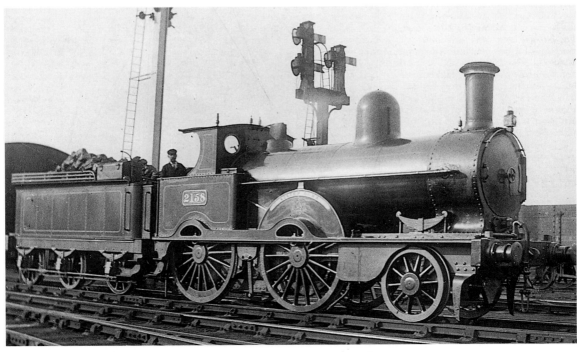

Below left There cannot be many women who had a railway locomotive named after them! Walsall's nursing heroine, Sister Dora, did, and the locomotive in question was a frequent visitor to the town, usually on the anniversary of her death. A photograph of the locomotive was irresistible, bearing in mind the importance of her memory and her statue in the centre of the town. The LNWR's No 2158 was a 2-4-0 'Waterloo' Class loco designed by F. W. Webb and entered service in the early 1890s with the name *Serpent*. Later renamed *Sister Dora*, it is seen here at Bescot Shed in about 1903, about to work on a Birmingham local train. In later years, to continue the tradition, a Class 31 diesel-electric loco was also named *Sister Dora*. *R. S. Carpenter*

Above Beyond the railway station at the top of Park Street is Townend Bank, with Wolverhampton Street going off to the left, and the tram tracks to Willenhall and Green Lane to the right, which took the curve into Stafford Street behind the four men standing on the pavement on the right. Tramcar 17 has just left Park Street on its way to Bloxwich in about 1904. The shadow on the left of Park Street is that of Walsall's other theatre, The Grand. Behind the tram is Her Majesty's Theatre, which was only four years old when this tram trundled past. The theatre was replaced by the Savoy Cinema in 1936, which later became the anonymously named ABC. The site is occupied today by a large Woolworth's store, while to the extreme left, in Wolverhampton Street, is the new Walsall Art Gallery. *Commercial postcard*

Bradford Place

The way out to the west of the town from The Bridge, towards Darlaston and Wednesbury, was by way of Bradford Street, which came into the town centre by way of a hill that passed the Walsall & District Hospital founded by Sister Dora in 1878, but which was actually opened after her death. At the bottom of the hill there is a triangular area, known as Bradford Place, which was for many years bounded on the

west side by the Midland Railway goods sheds and on the north side by a similar LNWR building. Much of this latter area was used when the Saddlers indoor shopping centre was built. Alongside it is the tall Gothic-styled Science & Art Institute, which was opened in 1887 and is still in use today.

In the middle of Bradford Place is the town's war memorial, which was placed there to commemorate the killing of the Mayoress in 1916 by a bomb dropped from a German Zeppelin airship. Bradford Street then passes through a narrowing funnel of premises built in the last decade of the 19th century before emerging into the open space at The Bridge. Bradford Place was, after the closure of the tram services to Darlaston and Wednesbury, always the preserve of motorbuses, as the tram services were not, in this part of the town, converted to trolleybuses.

Above Looking from the horse trough, suitably inscribed 'For Gods Creatures', in Bradford Place in about 1910, in the distance, at The Bridge, is one of the South Staffordshire top-covered trams, possibly Car 36, which is working on the Darlaston service. It is recognisable as a South Staffs car by the position of the destination box, which was mounted above the motorman's head in the vestibule. The Company was allowed to operate over Walsall Corporation tracks from 1 May 1907. The other four distant trams all belong to Walsall Corporation and are from the Brush-built 1-28 class, although each is different. On the right is one of the short Magrini-topped trams covered in 1906, while next to it, on the left, is one of the six Milnes-Voss 'Balloon' totally enclosed cars whose top deck was covered in 1904. Just visible to the left of the South Staffordshire tram is one of the flat-canopied top-covered trams, while to the left of the clock is one of the trams in its original condition. On the right of Bradford Street is the rather splendid tiled-fronted Turf Tavern public house, while beyond it is the 15-bay stucco 1890s building with the upper walkway, a unique survivor in the West Midlands. Between the two are the premises of the India & China Tea Company; most tea and coffee sellers have long since disappeared, but one such shop, W. Snape, still thrives in Wolverhampton today. *Commercial postcard*

Below left About 90 years later, on 29 January 1999, a bright yellow Pete's Travel bus loads up in Bradford Place when working on a commercial, rather than tendered, shortworking service on the 401E route to Yew Tree Estate on the border with West Bromwich. Pete's Travel and Lionspeed were set up by Peter Jones after the Conservative Government's deregulation of bus services in 1986 and now has a large network of services in the Birmingham, West Bromwich and Walsall areas and a fleet of just over 90 single-deckers. S401 HVV, a leased Dennis 'Dart' with a low-floor East Lancs B44F body, is at the time of writing one of about 25 of the popular 'Darts', which in this fleet, together with the East Lancs examples, have vehicles bodied by Wright and Plaxton.

The buildings behind the bus, with the exception of the new Brewers premises, are, above ground level, largely unaltered since 1910. Even the Turf Tavern has reverted to its original name, while the walkway balconies over the Digbeth Arcade have been carefully restored. From the no entry signs on the left, the bottom end of Bradford Street has been redeveloped in conjunction with the building of the Saddler's Shopping Centre. *D. R. Harvey*

Two bus drivers wearing winter coats stand in Bradford Place in 1938. In front of them is Dennis petrol-engined bus 25 (DH 7552), an H-type built in early 1929 but heavily rebuilt in 1933. In its new form its body was virtually a replacement of the original built by Shorts to the design of M. J. Somerfield, who later became the Corporation's General Manager. It is working on a short working to Pleck about 2 miles away on the 38 service to Darlaston, during its last year in service.

Behind the Dennis is the former demonstrator, 60 (DHX 504), a 1936 AEC 'Regent' 661 with a Park Royal H30/26R body, which is working on the 38 service to Darlaston. Pulling in behind the AEC, beneath the imposing Science & Art Institute, is the other former Commercial Motor Show exhibit of 1936 in the form of

Leyland-bodied Leyland 189 (ATE 222). Beyond the distant bridge carrying the railway over Bridgeman Street are the iron foundry and rolling mill chimneys that served the factories on the Pleck Road.

On the left is the open space on which stands Walsall's War Memorial. This is being passed by a Morris Fourteen of the type introduced in 1938 that had a painted radiator shell. This site was chosen as it was here, on 31 January 1916, that Mrs Slater, the Lady Mayoress of Walsall, was fatally injured. She was returning from Pleck on balloon-topped tramcar 16 when a bomb dropped from a Zeppelin airship exploded in Bradford Place just as the tram was passing. The War Memorial was placed there in her memory. *Walsall Local Studies Library*

Below The first Walsall/West Bromwich joint bus service began on 1 January 1926 when the 14 route to West Bromwich via Fullbrook was begun. Single-decker buses from both Corporations were used, with a half-hourly frequency, until the mid-1930s, when it was converted to double-decker operation. West Bromwich initially used its small bus, 8 (EA 2490), a 14-seat, Dixon-bodied Morris, while Walsall used its only small-sized bus, 38 (DH 4782), a Guy OND. The popularity of the new service quickly meant that 32-seater Dennis Es entered service. One of the latter, 93 (DH 6424), with a rather old-fashioned-looking Vickers B31R body, stands at the Bradford Place terminus of the West Bromwich service in 1932, at the Bradford Street end of the bus shelters. The ornate, wrought-iron bus shelter is impressive, but not exactly storm-proof, as it is open on three sides. The Bradford Street depository was on the corner of Bradford Street. *R. L. Wilson*

Bottom There was always a mobile canteen parked in Bradford Place in post-war years. Standing alongside the wall of the War Memorial and plugged into its own electricity supply is a 1935 Dennis 'Ace', which had been 109 in the bus fleet. Registered CDH 37, this Park Royal-bodied 20-seater was the last of a trio of these pretty little buses, nicknamed 'Flying Pigs' because of their blunt-snouted bonnets, that entered service in 1935. It was withdrawn at the end of the war and was converted to a mobile canteen, in which capacity it lasted until 1961 when it was replaced by the cut-down Guy 'Arab' glimpsed in the next photograph. Of the other two Dennis 'Aces' built in 1935, 107 was exported to Belgium's Economic Mission, to help with the desperate transport situation after the war, and 108 had a more prosaic 'after-life as Walsall's ticket van. With its radiator muff, portable wooden steps at the rear and the crate of sterilised milk 'at the front door', the mobile canteen was something of a home-from-home for the bus crews. *R. F. Mack*

Opposite top Post-war the bus shelters in Bradford Place are now cantilevered from the wall of the Science & Art Institute, offering intending passengers a little more protection from inclement weather. The bus working on the 37 service is 6 (2736 DH), a 1964 rear-engined Daimler 'Fleetline' CRG6LW with a Northern Counties front-entrance body. This was one of the designs developed by that most idiosyncratic of General Managers, Ronald Edgley Cox. They were only 27ft 6in long, and despite their shortened front overhang still managed to squeeze in (literally) 70 seated passengers. The 37 was the clockwise circular route from Bradford Place, Walsall, that went to Wednesbury and Darlaston before returning to Walsall, while the 38 service did the same journey only anti-clockwise.

Just visible at the end of the row of shelters is the single-deck mobile canteen, cut down from wartime double-decker bus 221 (JDH 33). This Guy 'Arab' II was quite an early example of the model, entering service in 1943 with an 'utility' body built by Park Royal. *R. Marshall*

Opposite middle Standing alongside the War Memorial is one of the many 'one-off' buses purchased during R. Edgley Cox's long tenure, which must have made maintenance and spare parts a nightmare, but gave Walsall Corporation a reputation amongst enthusiasts for every bus coming around the corner being something different. This example, 821 (TDH 673), was a Daimler CVG5, and quite unusual for 1954, as by that time most CVGs entering service were fitted with the larger 8.6-litre six-cylinder

Gardner 6LW engine and not the smaller five-cylindered 7.0-litre 5LW unit. 821 was exhibited at the 1954 Commercial Motor Show, where it was in company with the next two new buses in the Walsall fleet: 822, the second AEC 'Regent' V to be built, and 823, a Leyland 'Titan' PD2/14. 821 was fitted with a 65-seater Northern Counties body of pleasing proportions and entered service in October of the same year, lasting for 19 years, well into West Midlands PTE days. It is waiting to run on the regular Bradford Place service to Darlaston and Wednesbury. *Vectis Transport Publications*

Bottom The early years of West Midlands PTE showed little change in Walsall's indigenous bus fleet. The application of Fablon fleetname stickers to the by now unrelieved pale blue livery was the only clue to the change of ownership.

Here 829 (WDH 904) is leaving the Bradford Place terminus and is in Bradford Street on its way to Wednesbury. This was one of the 826-840 numbered batch of Daimler CVG6s delivered in the early spring of 1956 and again showed the General Manager's willingness to adopt new ideas. These 15 buses were built to the same specification as a well-known Daimler demonstrator, SDU 711. They all had Twiflex couplings that enabled the usual fluid flywheel to be replaced with a conventional friction clutch while retaining an automatic gear selection. Daimler's intention was to try to woo orders from the BET Group of companies, which was wedded to synchromesh gearboxes and rarely ordered Daimlers. It was hardly a success and the Walsall order represented the largest, if not the only, batch to be built.

In addition, their Willowbrook H37/29R bodies were built to a 'low-highbridge' height of 14 feet. This was done by building the body directly on to the chassis frame with outrigger supports and not using the usual body underframing, and the lower body height is indicated by the way the top of the driver's cab door intrudes into the panels between the decks. Behind 829 is the public house that at the time was known as the Tavern In The Town, but which has since reverted to The Turf Tavern. *A. J. Douglas*

St Paul's Street and Bus Station

St Paul's Street originally ran from Wiseman Street and parallel to Park Street, to the south-west, but in later post-war years the road was realigned to be a continuation of Townend Street. The road crossed the railway line by means of a rather attractively balustraded bridge and dropped down the hill towards the late-Victorian St Paul's Church, opposite which had been the site of the Walsall Blue Coat School from 1859 until 1934 when it moved to Springfield Road.

After the site was cleared the newly created open space became Walsall's main bus station, which gradually came into use during 1937. With its impressive loading platforms, brick passenger shelters and huge wooden route boards, it remained largely unaltered until 1955 when trolleybuses, which since 1950 had loaded only at the shelters actually in Park Street, were allowed into the Third Platform. Until this time all buses had entered at the top of the hill, but the introduction of trolleybuses meant that they all left by the northern route towards Townend. Subsequent rebuildings of St Paul's altered the direction of the buses coming into the bus station and at the time of writing is being totally rebuilt by Centro, which controls the operation of bus services in the West Midlands area.

St Paul's Street contained the Transport Department's main town centre offices, which were situated in the bell-towered building at the top end of the bus station. Opposite the bus station the Corporation occupied an area of waste ground on the corner of Hatherton Road where were parked buses whose crews were having a break between duties.

If the headquarters of the Wesleyan & General Assurance Company in Steelhouse Lane, Birmingham, were impressively grand, those in Walsall, occupying an early-19th-century building on the corner of St Paul's Street and St Paul's Close, looked comfortably reassuring. Beneath the Georgian cornice windows stands Sunbeam MS2 trolleybus 218 (HDH 213) as its driver looks back up the street towards Townend. This was one of the last four pre-war trolleybuses to enter service with the Corporation on 1 March 1940.

All of Walsall's pre-war trolleybuses were six-wheelers, whereas after this quintet was delivered the Corporation only bought one other six-wheeler. The four, numbered 216 to 219, were attractively bodied by Park Royal to a design that had been developed for Huddersfield Corporation. The bus is carrying its post-war number of 320, which it received in 1950, but looks in dire need of a repaint. It is working on the 30 service from Bloxwich, after the inbound trolleybuses had been re-routed from Park Street. *R. A. Mills*

Above Despite their age, the five Weymann-bodied Sunbeam MS2s were repainted in 1951, and 166 (ADH 12) was renumbered 312 to become the last of the 1933-built six-wheelers to remain in service; it was withdrawn at the same time as the much later EDH and HDH-registered Park Royal-bodied MS2s on 30 September 1956.

Looking positively sparkling, 166 stands under the trees at the bottom of St Paul's Street, having worked in from Bloxwich on the 30 service. Beyond the Wesleyan & General premises at the top of the hill, near the railway bridge on the corner of St Paul's Terrace, is an open space; once occupied by old houses, by the early 1950s it was being used to park a few cars, including an SS Jaguar and an Austin Fourteen. A few years later Walsall Corporation used the area for parking buses between turns. St Paul's Church, completed in the Decorated Gothic style in 1893, was never completed to its original spired form; the proximity of Walsall Brook and the high level of the underlying water table made the ground unable to support the extra weight of a spire. The on-going occupation of raising church restoration funds was again in full swing, the notice announcing that '£5,000 needed to repair this church'. *R. Hannay*

Above right It must have been something of a shock to the passengers on the Bloxwich trolleybus service in the spring of 1953 to see an orange, green and cream-liveried double-doored, single-decker, which apparently had very few seats but a lot of grab-rails for 'standee' passengers. Having been demonstrated previously to Nottingham Corporation, not even Mr Edgley Cox could persuade the folk of Walsall that this was their trolleybus of the future. Glasgow Corporation's TBS2 (FYS 766) had a BUT RETB1 chassis, usually reserved for export orders, and an East Lancashire B27D body, and was originally allowed to carry 40 standing passengers, although this was later reduced by ten. TBS2 waits at St Paul's Church in front of 333, formerly 237 (JDH 434), a Roe-bodied Sunbeam W built in 1946. *D. R. Harvey collection*

Below One of Short Brothers' few forays into bodying trolleybuses was the 160-164 batch mounted on Sunbeam MS2 chassis, which entered service on 1 October 1933. Eighteen years later 163 (ADH 9) is still having to pound its way through Leamore and on to Bloxwich on the 30 service. It is parked at the bus shelters alongside St Paul's Church not long before it was renumbered 309 in about 1949. The Short body, with its faint hint of a 'piano-front' style between the decks, looks a little rippled around the between-decks panelling, suggesting that beneath the surface the wooden framing is beginning to rot away. The following year the five Short and the similar-looking Beadle-bodied vehicles were withdrawn from service to be replaced by the same number of four-wheeled Brush-bodied Sunbeam F4s. *S. E. Letts*

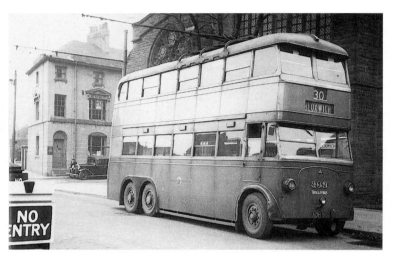

Bottom After 1950, when the in-bound trolleybuses were diverted into the town via St Paul's Street, the trolleybuses left the setting-down stop outside St Paul's Church and turned right into The Bridge, before leaving the town centre via Park Street. After 1955 the loop via The Bridge was abandoned, and for the first time since 1892 the centre of Walsall was devoid of electric traction.

In 1955 all the trolleybus services, with the exception of the Wolverhampton route, were diverted into the bus station. The Corporation installed a wiring loop opposite Darwell Street so that the trolleybuses could turn through 180 degrees and gain the bus shelters while facing up the hill and out of the town in St Paul's Street. Here Sunbeam F4 335 (NDH 952), a 95hp BTH electric-motored Brush-bodied trolleybus built in 1951, makes this 'arm-wrenching' manoeuvre when working on the 32 service to Lower Farm Estate in about 1963. *D. R. Harvey collection*

Above Early views of St Paul's Bus Station are unusual, and this splendid scene, dating from within months of its 1938 opening, shows that when it was built it was quite big enough for both bus traffic movements and the loading and unloading of passengers. Each of the four platforms was amply signposted for the most myopic of intending travellers and the shelters, at least for the period, really did offer waiting folk some measure of protection. In the bus station on Platform 4 are two Midland Red Metro-Cammell-bodied FEDDs dating from 1936, which are working on the 118 service to Birmingham. On Platform 3 is Walsall Corporation Dennis 'Lance' II 173 (EDH 301), with a Park Royal body dating from 1937, which is working on the 5 route to Brownhills. On the left is 1936 Dennis 'Lance' II 127 (DDH 333), which is about to leave for the Bell Inn on Birmingham Road and is being overtaken by a similar Dennis working on the 13 service to Streetly. At the top of the bus station, in the shadow of the Transport Department offices whose entrance was actually in St Paul's Street, are three more Park Royal-bodied Walsall double-deckers, while on the extreme right, parked outside St Paul's Church, is a Dennis 'Ace', a model better known by its affection nickname 'Flying Pig'. *Walsall Local Studies Library*

Above right On 21 July 1997 the bottom area of St Paul's Street is still recognisable. The old Transport Department offices are still there, although the alignment of the bus stands had been altered. Behind the clock tower is the multi-storey block rising above the Quasar Centre. By this date the Walsall to Wolverhampton service was running into the bus station, and the successor to the 29 trolleybus service became the 529 route after West Midlands PTE took over bus operation from Walsall Corporation in October 1969. In 1997, by now operated by Travel West Midlands, the 529 was converted to LPG-powered, route-dedicated, single-deck Volvo B10Ls with Alexander B43F bodies, which entered service in June 1997. Here 1510 (P510 KOX) is about to turn into the bottom end of the bus station. On the left are earlier vehicles that were purchased by West Midlands Buses; the MCW 'Metrobus' I double-decker with an MCW H43/30F body is 2135 (GOG 135W), while the single-decker is 1145 (G145 EOG), a 49-seater Leyland 'Lynx'. *D. R. Harvey*

Below Looking from the front of the Transport Offices into St Paul's Bus Station, we can see just how informative were the bus destination notice-boards that graced both ends of each of the four platforms. The Blakenall circular services – the 15, which ran anti-clockwise via Bloxwich, and the 30, which ran clockwise – were introduced on 6 June 1955 and went into Platform 3, as there was no room left on the loading stands on Platform 4 in St Paul's Street. Trolleybus 336 (NDH 953), one of the attractive Brush-bodied Sunbeam F4As of 1951, still painted in its original pale blue livery with a dark blue waistrail and dark blue upper saloon livery bands, leaves Platform 3 in about 1957 with a full load of passengers. The vivid acceleration of trolleybuses would discourage anyone attempting to jump aboard after the vehicle had moved away from the stop! *A. D. Broughall*

Bottom In 1955 the first of the 30-foot-long Sunbeam F4As were delivered, intended to replace the last of the pre-war six-wheeled trolleybuses as well as to enlarge the trolleybus fleet. The five remaining Weymann-bodied Sunbeam MS2s of 1933 were withdrawn almost immediately after a long and honourable career, but the six Park Royal-bodied Sunbeam MS2s of 1938 and 1940 remained in service until the last of the seven XDH-registered F4As arrived in the late summer of 1956.

It is therefore quite unusual to see a photograph of the 'old and the new' together. No 189 (EDH 863), one of the pair of 'Huddersfield'-styled six-wheelers of 1938 and by now renumbered 316, stands at the shelters in St Paul's Street; despite its imminent withdrawal it looks in remarkably good condition. Behind it is 862 (TDH 912), one of the new Sunbeam F4As that had entered service in June 1955. This trolleybus is now beautifully restored and runs a regular weekend service at the Black Country Open Air Museum in Dudley. At the bottom of the hill, in front of another turning F4A, is the short tree-lined section of St Paul's Street that leads to The Bridge. *R. Marshall*

Right Buses also used St Paul's Street, and in the late 1960s the last of the five 30–foot-long AEC 'Regent' Vs fitted with Willowbrook H41/31F bodies, 900 (MDH 900), working on the 1 service to Hednesford, has left The Bridge and speeds past the loading trolleybuses waiting in the very busy Platform 4. On the left trolleybus 863 (TDH 913) has just unloaded and its driver is talking to a colleague through the open cab door. The rear view of these Willowbrook-bodied vehicles shows the louvre above the fixed rear window next to the lower saloon emergency exit; this covered a gap at the top of the fixed window pane, which helped to ventilate the rear platform. *L. Mason*

Below After the West Midlands PTE take-over, it became apparent that the Walsall trolleybus system could not survive. By March 1970 30 former Birmingham City Transport Guy 'Arab' IV buses had been transferred to Walsall so that the first stage of the abandonment could take place. This occurred on 16 February 1970 in a somewhat surprising manner. Trolleybuses were withdrawn but there was no reduction in route mileage, which meant that the services were being operated by trolleybuses and the replacement former Birmingham buses, which were older than the trolleybuses they were replacing! Standing in St Paul's Street, 2564 (JOJ 564) is working on the 32 Lower Farm Estate service on 28 March 1970 and is being followed by ex-Walsall Corporation trolleybus 860 (TDH 910). The bus station was still being operated on a 'two-up and two-down' platform basis. Rather like the trolleybuses and the bus station, the buildings behind belonging to Marks & Spencer and F. W. Woolworth, which ran through to Park Street, were rapidly coming to the end of their working lives and within a few years this scene would be radically different. *J. H. Meredith*

Above Walsall Corporation did not have exclusive use of St Paul's Bus Station, as for many years Midland Red used the bottom end nearest to the church for its 118 service to Birmingham via The Scott Arms at Great Barr. Here SOS FEDD 2345 (FHA 849) waits at Platform 4 in about 1952; its Brush front-entrance body has been rebuilt by the Aero & Engineering Company (Merseyside) of Hooton with rubber-mounted windows in the upper saloon.

The young lady, in her 'New Look'-length coat, is looking towards the bottom end of St Paul's Street and into The Bridge. In the background in St Paul's Street are the one-way trolleybus wires introduced in 1950. The car in St Paul's

Close is an Austin Heavy Twelve-Four of about 1934 vintage. There is another FEDD behind 2345, while at the top end of the bus station is one of the full-fronted Park Royal-bodied Leyland 'Titan ' PD2/1s, which entered service with Walsall Corporation in 1951. *R. T. Wilson*

Below left Walsall Corporation ran a large percentage of its bus services outside the boundaries of the town, some going considerable distances to places that were not served by other operators. The long 23 service to Brownhills via Walsall Wood left the bus station at the bottom of Platform 3, near the back of Woolworth's store, in company with most of the bus routes to the north-east of Walsall.

Some of the last buses ordered by Mr M. J. Somerfield were two batches of buses bodied by Park Royal, which were some of the last composite bodies constructed by the company. He ordered 25 Guy 'Arab' IIIs, which were of the same chassis type as the 50 MDH-registered buses of 1949 but one foot longer at 27 feet, and 25 Leyland 'Titan' PD2/1s. The bodies were fitted with full fronts and were virtually identical other than their badges, although they could be distinguished from each other as the front wings on the Leylands were much nearer the front panel. 'Titan' 127 (ODH85) waits next to the impressive bus station route board in the late 1960s. This vehicle would survive to pass into West Midlands PTE ownership. *R. H. G. Simpson*

Above Walsall Corporation also operated motor buses on several services to Bloxwich, which loaded away from the trolleybuses on Platform 1 at the top end of the bus station. Before the Second World War Walsall was one of the few municipalities to remain loyal to the products of Dennis Brothers of Guildford. Despite their rarity elsewhere, between 1931 and 1941 Walsall purchased 12 'Lance' Is and 70 'Lance' II double-deckers. After 1934 the Corporation only purchased two demonstrators, one from AEC and one from Leyland. One of the last low-radiatored 'Lance' II models to be purchased was 173 (EDH 310) of 1937, which had the Dennis four-cylinder 04 diesel engines and, like most of the others, a Park Royal H28/24R body. It is painted in the attractive light and dark blue pre-war livery and would be one of the first of the type to be withdrawn in 1949. Behind it, turning into the bus station platform, is a war-time Massey-bodied Guy 'Arab' II. *R. A. Mills*

Above right The last view of buses in Walsall's St Paul's Bus Station is of the penultimate pre-war 'Lance' II delivered to Walsall Corporation, 215 (HDH 166), built by Dennis Brothers as a demonstration vehicle and fitted with the latest Dennis 06 'Big Six'-type 7.58-litre diesel engine. It was delivered in late 1939 and received the normal Walsall Corporation-style Park Royal body. The tall, rather ungainly radiator always looked 'wrong', irrespective of whose body was employed, although the semi-streamlined lower dark blue livery band did mask the squashed frontal appearance. The bus is working on the 16 service to Lichfield and is standing at the top end of the bus station on Platform 3 in about 1948. The last Dennis 'Lance' II, 220, was also a demonstrator and was registered by Dennis as JPH 828 in Surrey. This was a very different-looking beast, having a full-front body and the Dennis radiator mercifully hidden behind an almost equally ugly slatted grill. *R. A. Mills*

Below In the very last weeks of Walsall's trolleybus operation, the buses ordered by Walsall Corporation to replace them on Saturday 3 October 1970 briefly ran alongside them. In September 1970 the last of the ex-Ipswich trolleybuses, 353 (ADX 191), overtakes a brand-new Daimler 'Fleetline' CRG6LX with a NCME H45/27D body. Behind the new bus is another of the former Metro-Cammell-bodied Birmingham Guy 'Arab' IVs. The new buildings on the left, above St Paul's Close, were built in the 1970s, but fortunately the more 'friendly looking' St Paul's Church and the buildings below Darwell Street remain. *L. Mason*

Bottom R. Edgley Cox had previously been the General Manager of St Helens Corporation, and was responsible for the purchase of the only AEC 'Regent' III RT types built with standard London Transport Park Royal-style bodies outside the capital. Fifteen were built in May to June 1950 and another 25 were delivered in 1952. It therefore came as no real surprise that in 1958, when the first of the LTE Leyland 'Titan' 7RTs were withdrawn, Edgley Cox managed to purchase five fairly new but redundant buses, which were basically Leyland-engined versions of those that he had purchased new when he had been in St Helens. They were numbered 201 to 205 in the Walsall fleet, and 204 (OLD 601), a 1954 RTL, formerly RTL 1492, was therefore a bargain when purchased at only four years old. It is parked in St Paul's Street north-west of the bus station on Sunday 23 May 1965 when working on the 35 Inner Circle service along the Broadway. The passing Ford Popular 100E on the other side of the road heading towards the town centre is almost opposite the open space on the corner of Hatherton Road, which during the week was usually occupied by buses lying over while waiting for their next duty. By this date the lovely old Wesleyan & General Assurance offices had been demolished and the site hidden behind a long set of advertising hoardings. *A. D. Packer*

Right This photograph shows the bus lay-over area on the corner of Hatherton Road, with 834 (WDH 909), one of the low-highbridge Willowbrook-bodied Daimler CVG6s delivered in March 1956, waiting for its next duty in company with another member of the same class and a short-length NCME-bodied Daimler 'Fleetline'. *C. Carter*

Below Having placed in service in 1955 and 1956 the first 30-foot-long double-deckers in the country (the Sunbeam F4A trolleybuses), R. Edgley Cox instigated in 1962 the design of a 25ft 7in Daimler 'Fleetline', which became Number 1 (I UDH) in the Walsall fleet, entering service in November 1962. The aim was to provide a more manoeuvrable rear-engined double-decker and this was achieved by shortening the front overhang and effectively placing the driver over the front axle. However, 1 UDH was just too cramped and in 1963 the first production short-length 'Fleetlines', by now stretched to 27ft 6in, were placed into service. Despite their short length, the Northern Counties bodies managed to accommodate some 70 passengers. Between October 1963 and February 1969 99 of these strange-looking buses entered service and could therefore claim to be Walsall's only standardised double-decker in the fleet! They were not quite unique as the superbly named Stalybridge, Hyde, Mossley & Dukinfield Joint Board (SHMD for short) ordered ten similar vehicles.

In pristine condition, one of these buses, 34 (EDH 634C), is parked on the waste ground opposite the Transport Offices when new in 1965. Parked next to it is one of the Dennis 'Loline' Mark IIs, purchased in 1960. It is 880 (880HDH) and at a full 30 feet long its Willowbrook body had a seating capacity of 74. Walsall purchased 17 of the 48 of the 'Loline' IIs built, and they proved to be the Corporation's last purchase from the Guildford-based chassis manufacturer. They also had five-speed constant-mesh gearboxes, which were very difficult to master! On the right is 960 SDH, a Ford Thames 15cwt Dormobile minibus that was used by the Transport Department for staff transport. *J. Cockshot*

Above Standing in Hatherton Road, another area used for lying over, is 52 (JDH 200), a wartime Guy 'Arab' II built in 1944 and fitted with a Massey UH30/26R body. The Massey body was one of the most uncompromising of the wartime MoWT-style body designs; with their deep roof, angular front and rear domes, Massey bodies were either long-lived, or withdrawn very early due to the use of unseasoned wood; although 52 looks in good condition, it was withdrawn in 1956, suggesting that its body belonged to the latter group. *R. F. Mack*

Below Buses arriving at Walsall from Aldridge came into St Paul's Street by way of Hatherton Road. On a gloomy day in about 1962 Walsall's only Leyland 'Atlantean' PDR1/1, 841 (841 PDH), delivered in September 1959 and for some strange reason specified with a low-height Metro-Cammell body, comes into the town centre on the 6 route. It is being followed by a Midland Red XHA-registered BMMO D7, which is working on the 115 service from Six Ways (Aston) and Great Barr. On the traffic island, as well as the 'Keep Left' bollards and the two concrete flower tubs, which were a token 1960s attempt to brighten up the town centre, there is a gravel bin that was vital in icy weather, for the climb up the hill from the right in St Paul's Street on the concrete road surface needed such a facility. *J. Cockshot*

Above The first Leyland Motors metal-framed body went into production in April 1934. It was a six-bay construction design known as the 'V-front', and was not very successful, being too lightly framed and suffering from bulkhead failures. A considerable amount of expensive remedial work had to be done by Leyland on vehicles that failed in service, which all but stopped body production at the South Works. A demonstrator, ATE 222, was built for the October 1935 Commercial Motor Show and was sold to Walsall Corporation in the following February. It was quickly repainted from its green and cream demonstration livery into Walsall's two-tone blue and is seen parked in Hatherton Road in about 1953 as the Corporation's 189.

Despite the body's poor reputation, 189 stayed in service until 1956. *R. A. Mills*

Below The Ministry of Health Medical Examination Centre occupied a rather utilitarian-looking building in Hatherton Road, outside which Guy 'Arab' I 5LW 179 (HDH 943) is standing. The bus has a correspondingly utility-style Park Royal body, and was built in 1943. Behind it is a Midland Red SOS FEDD, which has arrived in Walsall from Birmingham. Between the two buses are a number of people waiting for another; it looks as if they have just missed one, judging by the recent tyre tracks on the wet road surface. *A. D. Broughall*

Above Post-war single-deckers were not very prominent in the Walsall Corporation fleet and it came as something of a surprise when five Leyland-bodied and five Park Royal-bodied single-deckers arrived. Waiting in Hatherton Road alongside the Civic Centre is 802 (PDH 802), one of the Leyland 'Royal Tiger' PSU1/13s, fitted with a Leyland B44F body, which entered service in December 1952 and was originally ordered as a half-cab Leyland 'Tiger' PS2. Having an underfloor engine gave the vehicle extra seating capacity as well as, in later life, allowing it to be converted to One-Man Operation. By now with a few dented panels, the bus is parked – abandoned, even – in front of a Staffordshire-registered Morris Oxford MO Series car of 1950; it has worked in on the 17 service from Cannock. *S. N. J. White*

Below During the late 1960s the Quasar Shopping Centre was constructed at the top end of Park Street. The Walsall trolleybus system, although obviously coming towards the end of its life, was continuing to run efficiently despite problems with spare parts. Although the condition of many of their bodies left a lot to be desired, their mechanical condition was much better, and that largely forgotten item of trolleybus or tram operation, the overhead, was always well maintained.

Trolleybus 874 (GFU 692) speeds down St Paul's Street having come into the town from Blakenall on a 15 service. It was a BUT 9611T with a Northern Coach Builders body, and was new in July 1950 to Cleethorpes Corporation as their No 59. It was one of four of these trolleybuses purchased in July 1960, and the only one not to be extended to become a forward-entrance 30-foot-long vehicle. *A. B. Cross*

Above Walsall Technical College was built at the top of St Paul's Street near its junction with Wisemore Street and Townend. A reserved roadway was provided outside the college and this was used by incoming buses to set down passengers. Here a much-rebuilt 244 (MDH 329), a 1949 Guy 'Arab' III with a Park Royal body built in 1949, has come in from Brownhills on an 11 service. Like many of these 50 buses, the robust Guy chassis deserved better from the flimsy Park Royal body and most of them were rebuilt at Birchills Works with rubber-mounted windows. The expense of this rebuilding work might not have been necessary had the original body specification not been so parsimonious! *Photobus*

Above right Having worked on the 1 service from Rugeley, 897 (897 MDH) has unloaded its passengers at the top end of St Paul's Street outside the Technical College in 1966. The bus was one of the last 30-foot-long, front-engined double-deckers to be delivered to Walsall Corporation. Between July and September 1961, five Daimler CVG6/30s and five AEC 'Regent' V 2D2RAs arrived with Metro-Cammell 72-seat, forward-entrance bodies, while the last five 'Regent' Vs came with similar Willowbrook bodies. Once empty, 897 will be driven down the hill to St Paul's Street bus station, before loading up for the return journey to Bloxwich, Great Wyrley, Cannock, Hednesford and Rugeley. It is carrying an advertisement for one of Walsall's famous products, Highgate Mild Ale, which has been produced since the brewery was founded in 1898; after many years as part of the Bass Group, it regained its independence in 1995. The bus has left behind a motley collection of cars parked in the shadow of Dean's warehouse. These include a Standard 10, a two-door Morris Minor, an Austin Mini and a Minivan, while the pick-up van coming in from Stafford Street is a Bedford CA Mark II. *B. W. Ware*

A largely unaltered Sunbeam F4 trolleybus, 336 (NDH 953), fitted with a Brush H30/26R body, comes into the top end of St Paul's Street, with the junction of Townend and Stafford Street in the distance. To the left is where the Dennis E tower wagon, formerly bus 90 (DH 6421), is parked in the picture opposite. This time 336 is in no need of assistance! The ten of this class saw off ten of the 1933 Sunbeam MS2s when they were delivered in October 1951, the first one, 334 (NDH 951), having been exhibited a year earlier at the 1950 Commercial Motor Show. *D. R. Harvey collection*

Townend

Townend is situated at the top end of Park Street beyond the railway station. A bustling area of small shops, warehouses and back street workshops, the area was for many years dominated by the late Victorian Her Majesty's Theatre, which in its time had been the largest theatre in the town. The large open space in front of the theatre was known as Townend Bank, and in earlier years had been used for fairs and market stalls. Although it was a continuation of the town's main shopping street, Townend was never an area occupied by 'town centre'-type shops. Virtually the only old building to remain in the area today is The Red Lion public house, built in 1896 and a real gem of Victorian pub architecture.

The whole of the area was redeveloped in the 1970s, the area between Park Street and St Paul's Street being covered by the Quasar shopping centre. The old theatre was replaced in 1936 by the splendidly Art Deco Savoy cinema, the site of which today is a Woolworth's store.

Leaving from Townend were the main roads to the west and north of the town. Wolverhampton Street led past the wharves on the Walsall Canal and on to the Wolverhampton Road, while to the north is Green Lane, which went the direct way towards Bloxwich and is now the main A34 road. On the other side of the semi-circular Richmond's store was the entrance to Stafford Street, which led to Bloxwich by way of Leamore.

Townend also served as the original terminus for the Wolverhampton trolleybus service, which opened in 1931 and subsequently became an important part of the town's trolleybus operations.

Right The complicated road junction known as Townend gave rise to a correspondingly complicated overhead wiring layout. Trolleybuses circled the ABC cinema, successor to the Savoy, which was used as the terminal loop for the Wolverhampton service, while the trolleybus service from Bloxwich entered St Paul's Street from Stafford Street, and the Cavendish Avenue service came into the Townend Bank terminus from Green Lane. The result was that on an area of land on the corner of Wiseman Street and St Paul's Street the Corporation frequently parked a recovery vehicle or a tower wagon.

A 1928 Dennis E, 90 (DH 6421), originally with a Vickers B31F body, was converted to a tower wagon in April 1938 and survived in this capacity until February 1960. It is seen here parked on the aforementioned plot of waste ground in about 1955. The car on the right with a broken nearside headlight is a 1936 Morris Ten. In the background are the distinctive brick chimneys of Deans warehouse, which occupied a position at the bottom of Stafford Street. *A. D. Broughall*

Below Almost dragging its offside life-rail on the ground is Sunbeam F4 trolleybus 340 (NDH 957). Walsall bought ten of these composite Brush H30/26R-bodied trolleybuses in October 1951, and half of the 95hp vehicles, including 340, lasted to be taken over by West Midlands PTE on 1 October 1969. The body on 340 seems in surprisingly good condition, as these products tended to have a propensity to sag after about 14 years' service. It is working on the 31 service from Mossley Estate and has turned from Stafford Street, where John James's television and electrical goods shop is situated, into Wisemore Street before turning right into St Paul's Street. The Austin Cambridge A60, Austin Mini-Countryman, Ford 'Anglia' 105E and early Ford Transit van date the passage of the trolleybus to 1965. *J. Saunders*

Above Trolleybus 852 (TDH 902), working on the 31 service from Mossley, inches its way around the corner into the short length of Wisemore Street in front of Hearnshaw's carpet shop. Following the trolleybus is a Ford Zephyr 4, of the type similar to the six-cylindered version made famous in the BBC TV series *Z Cars*. 'Come back Fancy Smith, all is forgiven!' The trolleybus is one of the 30-foot-long Sunbeam F4As with 70-seater Willowbrook bodies. These were nicknamed 'Goldfish Bowls' because of their ugly frontal appearance. Stafford Street, at the Townend Bank end of the street, is still lined with 19th-century retail premises, reflecting the trades of the small individual shop owners. *D. R. Harvey collection*

Below Walsall Corporation was able to purchase 12 wartime Sunbeam W4 chassis, with either Park Royal, Brush or Roe 'utility' specification bodies, and 324 (JDH 331), renumbered from 228 in 1950, was one of the four bodied by Brush. As with nearly all of Walsall's MoWT-style trolleybuses, it had its body partially rebuilt, in this case around the front dome windows, which were prone to leaking rain, hence the rubber mountings. The deep, longitudinal channel beneath the nearside windows is where the bamboo pole was kept that was used to retrieve recalcitrant trolley-booms if they came off the wires. The trolleybus, working on the Blakenall circular service, is leaving the town centre by way of the one-way system in Wisemore Street. *D. R. Harvey collection*

Above Constance Franconero had two No 1 hits in the British Hit Parade, one that made No 2 and two that reached No 3 between 1958 and 1962. When she made her second film, *Follow The Boys*, in which she starred, Connie Francis, as she had become, was the world's best-selling female vocalist. What she could not have imagined was that in a distant English industrial town, far away from the sunny climes of Hollywood, one of her film posters would be captured next to a wartime British trolleybus. Wolverhampton Corporation jointly worked the 29 service, and its 417 (DUK 17), a Sunbeam W built in 1945 and rebodied by Park Royal in 1952, is unloading in Wolverhampton Street on 19 May 1963, before running alongside the ABC cinema and turning into Townend Bank to load up in Townend Street on the other side of the cinema. *W. Ryan*

Above right The jointly operated trolleybus service between Walsall and Wolverhampton originally had its terminus in Townend Bank at the top of Park Street. For most of the 34 years during which the 29 service was operated the route used the Savoy cinema as an anti-clockwise terminal loop. This meant that the trolleybus service, in common with many others up and down the country, started in a back street before emerging into a main road route.

Beneath the impressive brick back-wall of the ABC in Townend Street was the trolleybus loading-up stand for the 29 route. It is here that two trolleybuses, one from each operator, await their passengers. The Walsall vehicle is 323 (JDH 30), numbered 226 prior to 1950, a Sunbeam W4 and one of the earliest, in fact the 30th, of the type to be built. It had a Park Royal UH30/26R body; which could be easily distinguished from other wartime trolleybus bodies by the angled cab side window, which married to the bottom of the windscreen most attractively. The Walsall and Wolverhampton Through Service was operated by an equal number of trolleybuses from each operator, although the half-way point at Willenhall was operated from each end by each operator as service requirements demanded.

Behind 323 is Wolverhampton Corporation's 623 (FJW 623), a 1950 Sunbeam F4 again with a Park Royal 56-seat body. This was basically a version of the former Ipswich Corporation trolleybuses that came to Walsall in 1962, but with an 8-foot-wide body. It is on an enthusiast's tour; chosen because it had recently been repainted. *W. J. Wyse*

Above The joint inter-urban trolleybus route between Walsall and Wolverhampton was withdrawn on 31 October 1965 because of the construction of the M6 motorway at Bentley. The bus service retained the number 29 and used the same loop around the ABC cinema, where 900 (900 MDH), a 1961 30-foot-long AEC 'Regent' V 2D2RA with a Willowbrook H41/31F body, is loading in Townend Street before embarking on the 7-mile journey back to Wolverhampton. It is working immediately after the closure of the trolleybus service, as the overhead wires are still in position. As if to emphasise that the rest of the Walsall trolleybus system was 'alive and kicking', Sunbeam F4A trolleybus 869 (XDH 69) is passing along Green Lane on its way to the bus station on a Cavendish Road service. *R. F. Mack*

Below On leaving the ABC terminus, trolleybuses were routed around Townend Street, then turned left into Wolverhampton Street. Behind the trolleybus is the local W. H. Smith warehouse on the corner of Shaw Street. Surprisingly, the buildings are still in existence at the time of writing and are used by a toy retailer trading as Kiddisave.

Walsall's General Manager, R. Edgley Cox, was a devotee of the trolleybus and obtained the legislative powers under the Walsall Corporation (Trolley Vehicles) Order Confirmation Act in 1953 to expand the system. By 1963 this had been largely completed, but in order to adequately service the new routes there was a need to trawl through other trolleybus operator's redundant vehicles. The first two vehicles were purchased from the Pontypridd system in 1956, but the first large batch of second-hand trolleybuses were eight former Hastings Tramways Sunbeam W4s purchased from Maidstone & District. Their arrival was necessitated by the extension of the Mossley Estate service to The Eagle public house on 20 September 1959. The composite Weymann H30/26R bodies were considered to be in good enough condition for them to enter service with Walsall as soon as their brown and cream livery could be replaced by Walsall's all-over pale blue. Formerly 37 in the Hastings fleet, 306 (BDY 812) entered service in Walsall on 1 October 1959, and is about to turn right into Wolverhampton Street in about 1960 working on the Wolverhampton service. *C. W. Routh*

Before the Ipswich Corporation trolleybus system closed on 23 August 1963, Walsall purchased eight of its 12 Park Royal-bodied Sunbeam F4s; the Suffolk municipality's last batch of trolleybuses, they were new in 1950. They were placed in service on Walsall's streets over a 15-month period from March 1962, when ADX 196 appeared as number 347.

The last of the ex-Ipswich trolleybuses numerically in the Walsall fleet was 354, (ADX 192), which is turning into Wolverhampton Street from Townend Street not long after re-entering service on 15 May 1963; however, it was destined to be the first to be withdrawn, four years later, after receiving severe accident damage. The ex-Ipswich trolleybuses always retained their original destination boxes, and as the word WOLVERHAMPTON would not fit horizontally, it was printed diagonally, which had a very amateurish and 'home-made' look about it; regular passengers on services operated by these trolleybuses could be readily identified as they all walked around with heads cocked to an angle of 45 degrees! *R. F. Mack*

Around Townend and off to Wolverhampton

The opening of the Walsall trolleybus system took place on Wednesday 22 July 1931, with the service from Townend Bank along Wolverhampton Road to the Walsall Borough boundary, then on to Willenhall. The joint trolleybus operation with Wolverhampton Corporation began on 16 November 1931 after the canal bridge in Horseley Fields had been lowered. Walsall Corporation bought just four trolleybus for the service; 151 and 152 were AEC 663Ts with English Electric H33/27R bodies, while 153 and 154 were Guy BTXs with Brush bodies that were also 60-seaters. AEC 152 (DH 8312) stands at the top of Park Street in Townend soon after the trolleybus service was extended to Wolverhampton. The vehicles were attractive-looking buses, but they did belong to the period of body design that gave the impression that at the drawing-board stage no one could decide what to do with the front. Thus bulges, rounded cowls and, in this

case, a plethora of ventilation slots were the order of the day. One wonders if the terminus was chosen at this point because of Mr Male's bacon sandwiches! *D. R. Harvey collection*

Left On 3 June 1951 314 (ADH 14), numbered 168 only a few months before, turns across Townend Bank and into Stafford Street, working on the 30 service to Bloxwich on the circular service to Blakenall by way of Leamore. The Weymann-bodied Sunbeam MS2 is fully loaded with passengers on this warm spring day, when nearly all of the half-drop windows have been fully opened. The trolleybus would remain in service until the end of February 1955. Waiting at the stop at the top of Park Street, on the right, is 126 (ODH 84), one of the full-fronted Leyland 'Titan' PD2/1s with Park Royal bodies. *V. C. Jones*

Below Seen again at the top of Park Street is 126 (ODH 84), one of the 25 Leyland 'Titan' PD2/1s delivered in the last months of Mr Somerfield's regime. It is about to work on the 35 Inner Circle service, which left the town centre at the top of Park Street and went for a meander around The Broadway, the equivalent to a ring road. There is a lot of bunting and flags on display, although the reason for these festivities 40 years on is rather lost, unless it was Walsall's response to the Festival of Britain which had opened a month earlier. Temporary 'Keep Left' signs, of the sort that one was supposed to 'spot' if one belonged to the 'I Spy' Club, have been placed at the entrance to Green Lane in an attempt to stop motorists vaguely wandering across Townend. Behind the bus to the right are the shops of the Warwickshire Furniture Company, who were offering easy terms on the 'Finest Quality Furniture', which at the time very few people could afford. Beyond the Central Piano Saloon is the Red Lion public house, while to the left of the Leyland is Park Street, which stretches away beyond the railway station entrance down the hill towards The Bridge. *V. C. Jones*

Above The Cavendish Avenue service was the last new route to open, on 2 September 1963, and Walsall's trolleybus system reached its maximum mileage of 18.86. The trolleybus turning across Townend Bank is 332 (JDH 433). Behind it is the Banks's Brewery-owned Red Lion pub that still exists today, and following the trolleybus is an Austin Mini of about 1963 vintage. The Warwickshire Furniture Company has been replaced by the New Day furniture store, although the message of SPECTACULAR SAVING SALE seems to have followed the furniture retailing trade through to the present day!

The sparklingly painted trolleybus shows that Walsall did occasionally overhaul and repaint its vehicles, and when Birchills paint shop did eventually get out its paint spray it could do a good job! Formerly 236, 332 was a Sunbeam W4 with a relaxed or semi-utility body built by Charles Roe. Roe bodies could usually be distinguished by the raised teak waistrail below the lower saloon windows. The windows in the front dome have been rebuilt, but basically the bus is much as it was when delivered in February 1946. The period of time between the opening of the Cavendish Avenue service and the withdrawal of 332 was just under 29 months, so it is quite unusual to see one of these trolleybuses on this service, which was usually more associated with the 'Goldfish Bowls'. *L. Mason*

Above right Coming into the wide open space of Townend Bank in 1963 is the prototype short-length Daimler 'Fleetline' 1 (UDH 1). The sum total of the traffic is a Morris Minor 1000, while in Stafford Street there is a retreating Standard Vanguard Phase II, a model introduced in 1953. Stafford Street took both bus and trolleybus routes out of the town centre through an area of late-19th-century shops and houses to Birchills, where the depot was situated, and on to Leamore and Bloxwich. To the right of the bus some of the mean and run-down three-storey Victorian shop premises have already been demolished. The Morris Minor is emerging from Wisemore Street, which led into St Paul's Street and was used by the trolleybuses to get to The Bridge, as by this time access to The Bridge by way of Park Street had long been abandoned. To the left of Richmond's kitchenware shop, dominating the top of Townend Bank, was Green Lane, which was the main A34 road to Bloxwich. *A. B. Cross*

Above The last major rebuilds that Walsall Corporation Motors undertook with its trolleybuses were those extending three of the four former Cleethorpes Corporation vehicles from 26 to 30 feet long. The one seen here, 877 (GFU 695), was a BUT 9611T powered by a Metro-Vick 115hp motor, which had entered service in the Lincolnshire town as 162 in September 1950. The four originally had NCB H28/26R bodies, which were similar to those being constructed by Eastern Coach Works in Lowestoft. This was because NCB's chief designer, Bill Bramham, had recently left ECW to join the Newcastle firm. Due to the effects of family death duties, NCB was forced out of the body-building industry later in 1950 and it was left to the parent company, Smith's Delivery Vehicles, to continue in production, making battery-electric vehicles.

Extended to H37/30F, 877 went into service on 15 January 1962, and is seen waiting at the Townend Bank terminus of the 33 service outside the same premises that in 1950 had looked so shabby, but which had been refurbished at least at the shop level. All these buildings would be swept away before the demise of the trolleybus system when work on the Quasar Centre was begun in 1969. *R. Marshall*

Below Unloading passengers is the former Ipswich Corporation Sunbeam F4 353 (ADX 191). This was the last stop before the terminus in Townend Bank, which was opposite Townend Street in Green Lane. The trolleybus is working on the recently opened Beechdale Estate 33 route and is parked next to the rather faded sign for the shoe shop owned by A. Hewitt. In front of the trolleybus is the edge of Richmond's kitchenware shop, which with the ABC cinema guarded the large open space of Townend Bank. *P. J. Relf*

Until the loop around the Savoy/ABC cinema was introduced, the 29 service entering Walsall came along Wolverhampton Street and turned around in Townend Bank before stopping just above the Red Lion pub outside the Warwickshire Furniture store. This involved pulling the trolleybuses around on full lock in front of Richmond's shop in order to reach the loading stops. The impressive Red Lion can be seen in the background behind the Ford Popular 100E parked next to the cinema canopy. Mercifully for the trolleybus drivers, this arm-wrenching loop was removed and the vehicles could gently glide around the cinema, albeit without passengers, which was a pity as they might have read the notice-boards about current and forthcoming attractions. The jointly operated trolleybus service meant that Wolverhampton trolleybuses were seen in Walsall and vice versa. Sunbeam F4 608 (FJW 608), a Park Royal-bodied trolleybus of 1949 vintage, turns left into Townend Street from Green Lane on 19 May 1963. *W. Ryan*

Stafford Street to Birchills

The character of the route out of the town centre, starting in Stafford Street then, beyond Proffitt Street, becoming Bloxwich Road, is one of rapid expansion. The nearby iron furnaces in Green Lane, the coal-mining in the Birchills area and the brick-making in the area on the townward side of the Wyrley & Essington Canal, gave this area a lot of trades. In the lower part of the tram route, in the side streets off Stafford Street, were metal-working shops, including brass-makers and finishers, wrought-iron working, metal casting, locksmiths and, in connection with Walsall's famous leather trade, chain and buckle manufacturers. The Stafford Street housing was the earliest and therefore the worst, and the area had a very cosmopolitan population even in the last decade of the 19th century, with Scottish, Irish and pogrom-fleeing Jews from eastern Europe. The heavy industry was more in the vicinity of Green Lane, so the Stafford Street area was limited to a domestic level of workshops and rows of terraced houses built from the 1850s to accommodate the workers.

Near the start of Bloxwich Road at Proffitt Street was the Walsall to Wolverhampton railway line, opened in 1872 by the Midland Railway. It passed beneath the road in a deep cutting, where there were a number of sand and clay pits. These supplied the large brickworks between Bloxwich Road and Green Lane. Beyond, in Bloxwich Road, was the former hamlet of Birchills, which had grown

In 1937 an Austin Ruby Seven overtakes a 1930 Birmingham-registered two-seater car and a Morris Eight van at the town end of Stafford Street. The leather merchants, including Hewitt's and, almost next door, Badam's, represent Walsall's most famous industry. This developed because tannin was extracted from the local oak woodlands, and locally slaughtered cows and sheep had their hides processed into leather. This led to the manufacturing of leather equine accessories and, in more recent years, high-quality leather goods of all sorts. Behind the cars and beneath the trolleybus wires is one of the 12 Dennis 'Lance' Is, which were delivered to Walsall in 1931 and remained in service until 1944, built with the exaggerated 'V'-plan front upper saloon windows that the General Manager, W. Vane Morland, employed on all the 1931 double-deck deliveries. He so liked this idea that when he left to become General Manager of Leeds City Transport in 1931 he took it with him and had AEC 'Regents' and Dennis 'Lances' bodied by Charles Roe to the same style. He also took the three cream-banded turquoise livery with him to Leeds. *Walsall Local History Library*

further after the completion of the Wyrley & Essington Canal in 1798. Birchills clustered around the canal, and alongside it, known locally as 'The Curley Wurley', were flour mills, small foundries and several narrow-boat building yards.

It was because of this rapid growth of the town out through Birchills and on to Leamore that the opportunity to introduce public transport was taken. On 4 December 1884, only 12 years after the area's only railway station had opened at North Walsall, steam trams came into operation from Walsall to the edge of Bloxwich.

Right The former Ipswich Corporation trolleybus 125, a 1950 Sunbeam F4, had been that town's last trolleybus numerically. It has just entered Stafford Street in Walsall, with Townend Bank in the background, and behind it are the pilastered and decorated premises of Richmond's and a row of late-19th-century buildings leading towards Bloxwich Road. This includes the Ansells public house The Criterion, which provides a contrast between the advertisement for its own Bruno bottled brown ale and the locally produced Highgate Mild Ale as advertised on the side of the trolleybus. Ironically, the Walsall brewery, founded in 1898 and taken over by Mitchells & Butlers in 1938, survives today as an independent brewer of CAMRA-recommended real ale, while Ansells, formerly of Aston Cross, one of the great old names of Birmingham's brewing industry, languishes as part of the Carlsberg-Tetley group and is now produced in Burton-upon-Trent. The trolleybus, ADX 195, now numbered 346 in the Walsall fleet, is working on the 33 service to the Dudley Fields Estate. It is being overtaken by a 12cwt Bedford CA Mark II van of 1964; with their semi-forward-control layout and sliding door, these were one of the most successful of the pre-Transit-style light vans. *R. F. Mack*

Right Stafford Street's character was one of transition from the impressive town centre buildings to the better-quality houses on Bloxwich Road. On reaching Littleton Street West, with the newly cut Court Way on the left in front of The Record Shop, Stafford Street's character became one of late-Victorian terraced domestic architecture with rows of small shops such as Allen's florist on the right lining the road.

Access northwards towards Bloxwich Road has been limited by only allowing trolleybuses to pass through, and it is this point that Sunbeam F4 342 (NDH 959) is passing. This trolleybus entered service in 1951 and was one of the last 26-foot-long F4s to be constructed before the Construction & Use Regulations allowed double-deckers to be 1 foot longer. It was subjected to one of Mr Edgley Cox's many experiments with trolleybuses by being extended to 30 feet long, supposedly using Bristol 'Lodekka' frames, although as the 'Lodekka' was a semi-chassisless design, the use of these parts is questionable. What is beyond doubt is that in its extended guise 342 seated 65 passengers in a bus that could always be identified by its white-rubber-mounted windows. This trolleybus now resides at the Sandtoft Trolleybus Centre near Doncaster. *J. Saunders*

Above De-wired trolleybuses were a fairly unusual occurrence; indeed, in certain fleets it was a disciplinary offence for drivers to dislodge their charges from the overhead. In February 1970, with the remains of snow lying in the gutters of Stafford Street, the inevitable passer-by stands and watches, no doubt to the irritation of the crew, as the driver struggles with the bamboo pole in his attempt to put the trolleypoles back on to the wire. Beyond the row of Victorian terraces is the tower of St Peter's Anglican Church, built in 1841 on the corner of Croft Street.

The trolleybus is 870 (XDH 70), a Willowbrook-bodied Sunbeam F4A, and careful examination reveals that the Walsall Corporation crests have been painted out by the orders of the new West Midlands PTE. None of the last 28 trolleybuses that survived until the final closure of the system

on Saturday 3 October 1970 were either painted in WMPTE's blue and cream livery or even received WM logos. *D. R. Harvey collection*

Below As the Ford 300E 5cwt Thames van waits at the Croft Street junction in Stafford Street, a trolleybus comes swishing along towards the Lower Farm Estate on the 32 service. This was Walsall's last new trolleybus route, opening on 2 September 1963. On a dull day, with its saloon lights switched on, the trolleybus, 340 (NDH 957), approaches Proffitt Street where the 15 service to Blakenall service turned off. It is a Sunbeam F4 with a Brush H30/26R body, which would have been about 14 years old at this time. Behind the trolleybus is the tower of St Peter's Church, the building well hidden by the notice-board advertising Benson & Hedges cigarettes. *R. Symons*

Above 'The tip that's setting the trend' is the advertising slogan on the hoarding for long-forgotten Bachelor cigarettes, which is being passed by wartime Guy 'Arab' II 222 (JDH 34), running down Bloxwich Road. This bus had been rebodied in 1950 with a 1936 Park Royal body that had originally been mounted on DDH 151, a Dennis 'Lance' II. These pre-war bodies extended the lives of some 26 wartime Guys, and 22 survived in service until 1963. The bus has just left the stop on the corner of Derby Street, south of Birchills garage, watched by the 'lollipop man' on the corner. *A. D. Broughall*

Below Having passed Birchills depot on its way into Walsall working on a 31 service from Mossley, Sunbeam F4A 857 (TDH 907) approaches Pratt's Bridge, which crossed the Wyrley & Essington Canal. The unusual concrete lamp standards on the central kerbing of this short section of dual carriageway in Bloxwich Road were unique in Walsall, although they were replaced soon after the abandonment of the trolleybus system as some of the redundant traction poles were utilised as lamp standards. Many are still in use in the Dudley Fields area, nearly 30 years after the system was abandoned. The entrance to Birchills depot is marked by the tower wagon glimpsed behind the trolleybus; this was used for repairing the trolleybus overhead. Behind the triangular tower of the Methodist Church, which in the mid-1980s became a warehouse, are the gabled roofs of the original tramcar sheds. *L. Mason*

Below This official photograph of trolleybus 166 was taken opposite the entrance to Birchills depot in Bloxwich Road at the very end of September 1933, before it had even been fitted with registration plates. Soon to become ADH 12, this bus was one of the long-lived Weymann-bodied Sunbeam MS2s with BTH electrics that had been ordered for the opening of the Bloxwich service. It was one of 15 trolleybuses purchased from Sunbeam for this conversion, but unlike the two earlier AEC 663Ts and the two Guy BTXs of 1931, which had slatted grills in the front panels, these later vehicles only had the vestiges of a radiator grill. This was still the period when trolleybus body designers did not know how to produce an uncluttered appearance below

the windscreen. The rest of the body design also looked strange; while most of the body looked up-to-date, the trolleybus would have looked a lot better and more modern had it been given a smooth curved front profile. Renumbered 312 in 1950, 166 achieved 22 years in service before succumbing to the two-axle, 30-foot-long Sunbeam F4As in 1955. *D. R. Harvey collection*

Bottom Looking towards the rise over Pratt's Bridge, trolleybus 340 (NDH 957) turns into Carl Street across the short section of dual carriageway in Bloxwich Road. The canal bridge was near the site of the old Albion Flour Mill. Flour was frequently being moved by canal narrow-boats,

but the bridge was better known for its boat docks. Two celebrated boatbuilders, Bowaters and Worsleys, had their yards just to the west of the bridge, where the post-war housing stands on the right.

The trolleybus, an as yet unmodified Sunbeam F4 of 1951, is negotiating the vagaries of the overhead wiring in a series of manoeuvres that will involve accelerating, coasting or even braking across particular sections of the overhead in order either to activate the automatic 'frogs' or not to blow the contactors in the cab, which would then involve resetting the circuit breakers. The driver of 340 appears to be making the turn without any difficulty and, indeed, with the trolleybus leaning slightly as it speedily makes the turn, with some aplomb. *R. Symons*

Birchills Depot

The original South Staffordshire Tramways steam tram route was opened to the Spread Eagle public house on the south side of Bloxwich on 4 December 1884 and the new depot at Birchills came into operation about June of the following year. Up to that time the steam trams had run from their existing depot at Wednesbury. After electrification on 1 January 1893, the same day as the services to Wednesbury and Darlaston, the depot at Birchills was used for some of the tiny 40-55 class trams. When Walsall Corporation took over the running of the line on 1 January 1904, they also became the owners of the tram depot, but had to use the tower wagon shed until a larger structure could be completed to house its new fleet of 28 open-topped tramcars. The Corporation's trams used the depot for the next 29 years, as well as garaging buses from 23 May 1915 when two Tilling-Stevens TS3s, DH 904 and 905, entered service.

The bus fleet continued to expand; the first double-deckers, with enclosed top decks, arrived in 1928. Trolleybuses were purchased for the Willenhall route, which opened on 22 July 1931, although the Walsall Corporation Act of 1925 had extended the existing 1914 Act to enable trolleybuses to operate. As the bus and trolleybus fleets expanded, the tram fleet dwindled, with the last tram route to Bloxwich closing down on Friday 29 September 1933. In July 1942 the garage was hit by incendiary bombs that destroyed seven Dennis 'Lance' buses, four of which were only four years old. Over the next three decades Walsall Corporation Motors continued to expand both its garage and its fleet of buses and trolleybuses. On 7 October 1954 the old tram buildings were partially replaced by a new trolleybus garage to accommodate the new fleet of trolleybuses. The Walsall Corporation fleet reached about 200 buses and 60 trolleys by the early part of the 1960s.

During the late 1950s the motorbus fleet was also enlarged with a wide variety of buses from a number of different

Turning from Bloxwich Road into Carl Street and Birchills depot in the late 1920s is Walsall Corporation tramcar 18. This was one of the original 1904 open-top trams that had been top-covered and vestibuled in about 1910, which at least gave the tram the impression of being up to date. The lack of any other traffic is noticeable, and emphasises how important the tram system was to the movement of people in the town. The only other road user is a lone cyclist.

A corner shop occupies the end of the 1880s-built terrace of houses. It has a chocolate vending machine by the bay window of the converted front room, and would have sold a wide variety of products ranging from items of grocery to sweets, tobacco and household goods such as bars of soap and cleaning materials. These little corner shops, often run by the lady of the house, were known as 'huxters' and survived throughout the country until the advent of the supermarket chains in the late 1960s. The houses themselves were for many years owned by the transport undertaking and were only sold to a housing association during the last four years of the West Midlands PTE. *J. H. Taylforth collection*

manufacturers. By the mid-1960s the Corporation began to standardise on short-length Daimler 'Fleetlines', which gradually encroached on the garaging facilities as the trolleybus fleet began to decrease. After the enforced closure of the joint trolleybus service to Wolverhampton due to the construction of the M6 motorway at Bentley, the trolleybus system remained the same size until the closure decision was taken by the West Midlands PTE. The final

rites were not completed until 2 October 1970, almost exactly one year after the Corporation had been absorbed into the PTE. This resulted in the considerable expansion of garaging facilities at Birchills. After the take-over, an overhaul facility for WMPTE was opened adjacent to the garage to serve the North Division of the PTE. The garage has since passed through the hands of various owners and in residence at the time of writing is Travel West Midlands.

Left Working on the 15 service from Bloxwich towards the town centre and drawing into the bus stop opposite the entrance to Birchills depot and garage is trolleybus 337 (NDH 955), a Sunbeam F4 with a Brush H30/26R body built in 1951. By this time, some 15 years later, the body of the trolleybus had been rebuilt with rubber-mounted glazing in the front of the upper saloon. On the other side of the road is the entrance to the depot – the overhead wiring leading into Carl Street is visible. The original offices of the South Staffordshire Tramways Company were at this time still standing at the entrance to the depot. *C. Carter*

Below left A 12-metre-long Optare XL of Choice Travel, R743 BUJ, speeds past Birchills garage working on the 'showcase' 171 service on 9 March 1999. The bus is one of a number of these low-floor Optares owned by Choice, and with their distinctive bright yellow livery they enable this independent fleet to compete favourably with Travel West Midlands. The 171 route from Walsall through Leamore to Bloxwich and on to The Eagle turning circle at Mossley is virtually the same as the trolleybus route that closed in 1970. Following the bus a Travel West Midlands Ford Transit pick-up is leaving the garage. The bus is passing the terraced houses that were always known locally as 'Depot Row' and which have been considerably renovated since their sale in the 1980s into private hands; the shop on the end has reverted to a house. The old Walsall Corporation offices have long since been demolished, and in recent years the large facility that was Walsall Bus Works has been opened and closed within the space of 20 years; the building is now used as a withdrawn vehicle store. *D. R. Harvey*

Right Standing at the entrance to Birchills depot is domed-roof tramcar 4, one of 15 trams fitted with uncanopied 'Magrini'-style top-covers in about 1905 and later re-topped with a full-length canopied, dome-roofed upper saloon. It is Whit Monday 1930 and this tramcar, despite looking in need of a repaint, would survive until the closure of the Wednesbury and Darlaston tram routes early in the following year. To the right of the tram, beyond Bloxwich Road, are the as yet unfinished semi-detached council houses in the Beeches Road area, which are so typical of municipal suburban development in the inter-war years. *D. R. Harvey collection*

Below The six Willowbrook-bodied Bedford SBOs of January 1956 led fairly quiet lives in and around the more rural localities in the Bloxwich area, and were all taken out of service in 1967 after attracting fairly little attention during their passenger-carrying days. Two of them, however, did have a long after-life: 297 passed to West Bromwich Welfare Department, and this bus, 298 (XDH 298), became the Transport Department's Mobile Canteen, surviving until 1973. It is parked in Carl Street in about 1959.

Behind it, lying abandoned, is 54 (DH 5505), a Dennis E of 1926, which had been rebodied in about 1935 by the West Bromwich coachbuilder W. D. Smith, with a rear-entrance, 32-seater body. In this form it outlived all the other Es in service by about five years and was then used as a towing vehicle, although how its puny petrol engine could tow anything seems surprising, as the poor old thing seemed to wheeze enough just hauling itself about! It was finally sold for scrap in October 1963. *L. Mason*

Above The prospect of mixing water with electricity might at first sight appear to be a recipe for disaster, but trolleybuses

had to be washed. Walsall was an early user of an automatic bus wash, and here trolleybus 870 (XDH 70) waits with its trolleybooms down before its turn through the wash in Birchills yard. It was usual for trolleybuses to go through on their traction batteries, but if the wash was not operating they would drive through normally. A look at the extra paraphernalia lying around to get to 'the parts that automatic washes cannot reach' is interesting. Hose pipes with attached brush-heads, mops and buckets are all in evidence, so despite the automatic wash the process was still a cold, wet, be-Wellingtoned labour-intensive operation. *D. Williams*

Left This is Car 16, the tram caught in the Zeppelin air-raid on 31 January 1916 when bombs exploded in Bradford Place. It was on its way from Pleck and unfortunately it caused the death of Mrs Slater, the Mayoress. Car 16 was one of the six Brush-built trams of 1904 fitted with Milnes-Voss 'white'-pattern 'Balloon' top-covers, and is standing in Birchills depot yard, with most of its panes of glass blown out by the blast.

These trams had been top-covered and totally enclosed before the Board of Trade Regulations that forbade narrow-gauge (3ft 6in) four-wheeled double-decker trams from being totally enclosed. The BoT's reasoning was that such trams would be more easily blown over on exposed routes than the apparently more stable trams working on 4ft 8½in standard-gauge systems. This restriction meant that the development of the four-wheel tram on narrow-gauge systems was left rooted in Edwardian designs. Narrow-gauge operators such as nearby Coventry Corporation were still receiving open-balcony four-wheelers from the Brush Electrical Company in 1931 as their 69-73 class. In 1921 Birmingham Corporation Tramways 'temporarily' converted two four-wheelers, cars 342 and 347, to act as prototypes for the next new batches of totally enclosed bogie cars to be numbered 637-661. These were also 'forgotten' and lasted in this condition until their withdrawal in 1950, whereas the six Walsall four-wheelers remained in service until 1931 when all the original tramcar fleet of 1904 was taken out of service. *Walsall Corporation Motors*

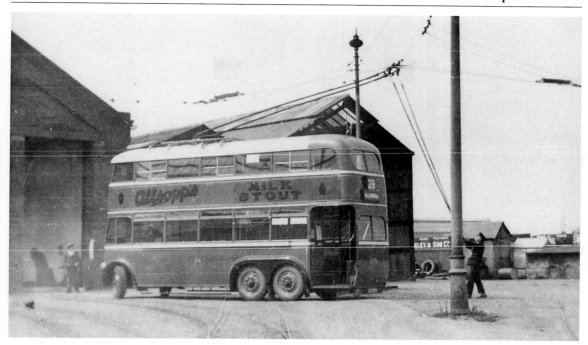

Above Walsall's first four six-wheeled trolleybuses could easily be distinguished from the 15 purchased in 1933 by having the lower saloon opening windows placed in the cant-rail panel in the same manner as a tram. This feature is visible on the Brush body mounted on Walsall's third trolleybus, 153 (DH 8313), a Guy BTX; this and 154 were the only Guy trolleybuses ever owned by the Corporation. It is being re-poled in Birchills depot yard by a driver who is apparently using two, not one, poles. This must have been not only quite a feat of strength but must also have required considerable dexterity! The neat rear end of these trolleybuses was quite a contrast to the uncertain design characteristics of the front end. Unlike some six-wheeled trolleybus designs of the period, the Guy BTX did have the advantage of having only one step on to the rear platform. *R. T. Wilson*

Below Parked at the rear of Birchills garage on 2 March 1938 are four Dennis Hs with heavily rebuilt Short bodies. The front two can be identified; on the right is 20 (DH 6309), while on the left is 18 (DH 6307). These buses had entered service in 1928 and originally had bodies built to the design of Mr Somerfield, which included an enclosed driver's cab and an enclosed rear platform and staircase. Unfortunately, their eccentrically styled bodies were quickly made to look antiquated and as a result the Corporation rebuilt them all between 1933 and 1934. The resulting bodies, based around the original Short Brothers body frames, certainly looked more modern, but alas the Dennis H chassis was, by the mid-1930s, no longer able to compete with more up-to-date chassis types, so later in 1938 all 17 Hs were taken out of use, despite all the money that had been lavished on them only four years earlier. *R. T. Wilson*

Above The original tramcar sheds at Birchills were always used by the trolleybuses, while the newer premises housed the motorbus fleet. Parked in the garage service road on 7 March 1954 is 233 (ODH 805), a Park Royal-bodied Leyland 'Titan' PD2/1, which was at this time only about three years old. These were among the last composite bodies – timber frames strengthened by steel flitch plates and covered with aluminium panels – to be built by Park Royal, while their full fronts rather hid the standardised body design. On the other side of the bollards in the yard is another 1951 vehicle, 340 (NDH 957), a Sunbeam F4 with a Brush H30/26R body; to the right is another trolleybus of the same class. Both trolleybuses and motorbuses were painted in the light and dark blue livery, which had a certain distinguished air about it that the later all-over blue livery totally lacked. *R. Knibbs*

Below A total of 22 de-licensed MCW 'Metrobus' Mk Is stand in Birchills yard on 9 March 1999. Those parked sideways on are next to the disused Walsall Bus Works, wherein there are more stored double-deckers and single-deckers. The nearest one is 2299 (KJW 299W), which had been allocated to Washwood Heath garage until that closed in the last months of 1998. The gabled building alongside which the remaining 'Metrobuses' are parked is the old tram depot, parts of which pre-date Walsall Corporation and go back to the steam tram days of the South Staffordshire Company. This link with the past must make this one of the oldest structures anywhere in the country to have been continually used for basically the same purpose. *D. R. Harvey*

Above Inside Walsall Works on the Birchills site in 1913 is car 32, one of four tramcars purchased from UEC with normal staircases and open balconies and vestibules. In this state the tram has yet to have its vestibules enclosed, which was done in about 1918. All tram operators had workshops that looked like this, and they were the hub of tram maintenance. The tram's body is suspended on trestles and its four-wheeled truck has been taken away for overhaul. In the foreground are traction motors and gear casings, which have been overhauled and are ready for replacement in other tramcars. *D. R. Harvey collection*

Below Birchills was clearly delineated into a bus garage and a trolleybus depot. The old tram depot originally housed the trolleybuses until 7 October 1954, when a new trolleybus 'garage' was opened, and in the gloom of this building are three identifiable trolleybuses. On the left, parked with its poles down, is 338 (NDH 955), a slightly rebuilt 1951-vintage Sunbeam F4 whose Brush H30/26R body has received rubber-mounted glazing in the upper saloon. Peeking through the steel support girders next to 338 is one of the ex-Ipswich Corporation ADX-registered trolleybuses, purchased in 1963. In the next bay are two of the 30-foot-long, Willowbrook-bodied 'Goldfish Bowl' Sunbeam F4As. The nearest is identifiable as the first of the 22 to be built, 851 (TDH 901), which is parked with its booms still attached to the overhead. Behind it is another trolleybus of the same batch, standing next to a portable staging that would have been used by the cleaning staff to reach the top deck. On the extreme right is a re-glazed Weymann-bodied former Hastings Tramways Sunbeam W4, registered in the BDY series. *Travel Lens*

Above Not too many bus operators had a mobile vacuum cleaner, but rest assured Walsall did! One of 25 Guy 'Arab' IIIs equipped with an 8.6-litre Gardner 6LW engine, 231 (ODH 308) entered service in 1951. These buses were bodied by Park Royal and had full-fronted 56-seater bodies. Withdrawals began in 1966, but 231 was converted to run from December 1967 as the mobile garage vacuum cleaner. With the two large fans mounted on the rear platform and the whole of the lower saloon effectively becoming the dust-bag, the Guy 'Hoover' Mark I survived in this bizarre capacity until the early days of 1973. *A. D. Broughall*

Below This strange-looking vehicle represents Walsall Corporation Motors' return to double-deck bus operation in 1928! If there was a competition to build the ugliest double-decker, one of the contenders would have to be the 17 Dennis Hs purchased by Walsall in 1928 and 1929. The H was very much a transitional chassis between the high-frame designs of the mid-1920s, which were fitted with outside staircases and 'solid' tyres, such as the AEC 504, and the later low-height Leyland 'Titan' TD1s and the AEC 'Regent' 661s of 1928 and 1929. The Dennis H was basically a double-decked version of the E-type single-decker. Although it had pneumatic tyres, it still had an antiquated side-valve petrol engine, a cone clutch, a right-hand gate-gearchange, a central throttle, an eccentrically raked steering wheel and no self-starter! This example, 21 (DH 7192), did have the advantage an enclosed staircase, but just look at those steps on to the rear platform! And there was another step to get into the lower saloon.

The body was built by Short Brothers and was perhaps one of their less inspired products, although their excuse was that it was designed by Mr Somerfield, Walsall's General Manager. The domed-roofed upper saloon did not extend over the cab and the front axle in order to keep the overall weight down, but despite this restriction the bus seated 28 passengers in the upper saloon and 24 in the lower. *Walsall Corporation Motors*

Above A not quite new Dennis 'Loline' II, 881 (881 HDH), of 1960 vintage, is parked next to an almost time-expired Guy 'Arab' II of 1945 in Birchills yard in 1961. The only tenuous connection between the buses is that both had extremely difficult manual gearboxes, which involved a lot of skill, dexterity and double-declutching.

Walsall's passing interest in the 'Loline' II model was yet another phase of the ever-active mind of Mr Edgley Cox. This was Dennis's new model, which the Guildford company had introduced in late 1959, and the Walsall General Manager's penchant for the novel meant that these low-floor, low-height vehicles were a most attractive proposition to him. If that appears to be a cynical view of his purchases, a quick examination of his vehicle ordering policy would explain the reason why Walsall became a bus enthusiast's delight!

Alongside the Willowbrook-bodied, forward-entrance 'Loline' is 37 (JDH 271). This wartime bus originally had a 'utility' MoWT-style Park Royal body, but in 1952 it was rebodied using a 1938 body that had been built by the same London-based manufacturer and had previously been mounted on 211, a Dennis 'Lance' II. Within a year the open-bonneted Guy would be withdrawn, having survived the travails of life in Walsall for 17 years, while the 'Loline', doomed as a model because of the new generation of front-entrance, rear-engined bus chassis, would only last for 12 years. *A. D. Broughall*

Below All four of the pioneering trolleybuses for the Willenhall service of 1931 managed to survive until the end of the Second World War. The Brush-bodied Guy BTXs 153 and 154 (DH 8313-4) were withdrawn after 14 years service in September 1945, while the AEC 663Ts 151 and 152 (DH 8311-2), bodied by English Electric and also 60-seaters, just made it into 1946, being withdrawn in February. Nominally replaced by the last of the wartime Roe-bodied Sunbeam W4s in the first three months of 1946, the four old six-wheelers were quietly towed away to the 'grasslands' at the rear of Birchills depot, where they would languish for about five years before their final disposal.

A comparison between the AECs and the Guys suggests that the English Electric bodies on 152, on the left, and 151 next to it, were both lower and had a more modern front profile when compared to the Brush-bodied Guys parked to their right. Unfortunately, the extreme amount of body framing decay on 152, still equipped with its wartime headlight masks and white edging paint, suggests that the two Brush bodies were marginally more durable than English Electric's. A sideline to these bodybuilders is that by 1931 both Brush and English Electric were struggling to keep their tram construction order books open and these trolleybus bodies represented another attempt by both companies to attract new orders from new markets. *R. A. Mills*

Above While the old trolleybuses languished in increasing rustiness in the secluded grassy wastes at the back of Birchills depot, the new generation, or what briefly purported to be that new generation, was proudly displayed in all its shininess on the front forecourt. One of Ronald Edgley Cox's first purchases was trolleybus 850 (RDH990), the last Sunbeam S7 chassis to be bodied by almost three years, as the chassis appears to have been built in 1950. It had been rumoured that the chassis had been lying in the Guy Motors works for a number of years before being purchased at a knock-down price by Walsall Corporation. It entered service on 17 September 1953, having been bodied by Willowbrook of Loughborough to the specification of Walsall's General Manager.

Mr Edgley Cox wasted no opportunity to experiment, and the body specified for 850 fulfilled this theme perfectly. The 30-foot-long trolleybus is seen when new at Birchills in its original incarnation. It was a two-door Pay-As-You-Board trolleybus à la London Transport's C3-type, 378 (CUL 378), which had been converted to a similar layout in 1945. Walsall's 850 had an H38/24D layout with a seated conductor's desk on the rear platform. After payment, the passengers could choose to stay in the lower saloon, where the rear platform could accommodate about 15 standing, or sit on the mainly longitudinal seating downstairs. The upper saloon was reached by a central staircase where the seating was laid out normally. The experiment did not really work, so in February 1961 the trolleybus reappeared renumbered as 350 with an H36/27R layout and the centre exit replaced by a normal window, but still retaining its centre staircase. It was withdrawn on 28 May 1967. *C. F. Klapper*

Left Standing at the exit from Birchills garage is the very first of Walsall's Dennis Es, 44 (DH 4905), one of 52 of this model that entered service with Walsall Corporation Motors between 1926 and 1928 and which became for a short while Walsall's standard single-decker. It was initially bodied by Vickers to a B32R layout, but was rebodied by the West Bromwich-based coachbuilder W. D. Smith and in this condition lasted until 1944. It is seen here with its original, rather old-fashioned body in about 1930. *R. Marshall collection*

Above No pictorial history would be complete without a photograph of the last trolleybus to operate in Walsall, even though this occurred under the auspices of the newly formed West Midlands PTE. A final procession carrying civic dignitaries included Sunbeam F4As 862, 864 and 872; the latter was Walsall's last new trolleybus, which had been fitted with a unique, non-standard Lockheed braking system from new. It was repainted for the occasion, and is seen undertaking the last rights on the evening of 3 October 1970. Suitably inscribed with the legend 'Walsall's Last Trolleybus', it was driven back to Birchills depot by Mr Edgley Cox himself. *D. R. Harvey collection*

Below Over the years Walsall Corporation had a variety of tower wagons, some of the earlier ones being converted from old buses. In later years they were usually purpose-built vehicles, based on smallish-sized lorry chassis. Two such vehicles are parked in Birchills yard. On the right is Karrier Bantam 706 BDH; this was a very long-lived model having been introduced in the early 1950s and remaining in production for nearly 20 years. On the left is 268 FDH, a Dennis Pax, which although a much newer design was less robust than the Karrier. Both tower wagons are equipped with crew-cabs and flashing orange warning lights mounted on the cab roof. *L. Mason*

Bloxwich

At first sight Bloxwich appears to be little more than a suburb of Walsall, but for generations it had been a totality in its own right. In fact, the settlement was set up in Anglo-Saxon times as Blocheswic, or 'Bloc's settlement'. The town stands on the northern edge of the West Midlands conurbation and historically marked the boundary between the rural agricultural landscape of Staffordshire and the coal-mining that developed in the 18th century. During the Industrial Revolution the settlement developed many iron-working domestic industries and the manufacturing of nails, needles and awls continued until it finally died out in the Depression of the 1930s.

The turnpiking of Stafford Road in 1766 meant that Bloxwich became an important point on the route between Walsall and Stafford, now the A34. The local canal was developed in the early 19th century to carry raw materials and heavy iron products, while the opening of the railway station in 1858 encouraged the town's growth.

The commencement of the South Staffordshire Tramways steam tram service on 4 December 1884 was perhaps even more significant. This opened up passenger transport for the working people of Bloxwich and linked the town to Walsall, Wednesbury and Darlaston by a regular public road transport service. By the first day of 1893, the whole 7½-mile route had been converted to electric operation, making it only the second system to be operated by electric overhead; the first was at Roundhay, Leeds, on 11 November 1891. The tram route to Bloxwich via Birchills and Leamore was the last Walsall route to close, on Friday 22 September 1933, and trolleybuses took over on the following day. The trolleybus service was extended in the 1950s to the developing Bloxwich housing estates at Dudley Fields, Mossley and Lower Farm as the system finally stabilised to a route mileage in the Bloxwich area of 12.69 miles. The trolleybus services lasted until the final closure on 3 October 1970.

On leaving Birchills, Bloxwich Road climbed a gentle hill towards Leamore. This was another small village, based around the Leamore Lane-Harden Road junction and quite separate from either Birchills or Bloxwich. Leamore has, therefore, its own urban structure and housing pattern.

Sunbeam F4A 854 (TDH 904) powers its way up the gradient of Bloxwich Road, using its 95hp motors to its optimum when working on the 31 service to Mossley Estate in about 1958. It has left far behind the substantial concrete bus shelter on the in-bound side of the road at the junction with Beeches Road, which so typified suburban Walsall, and has just passed Cope Street on the right and a row of late-Victorian bay-windowed housing on the left, which were contemporary with the original South Staffordshire electric tram route. Standing behind their street walls, these houses can still be identified today by their heavy white lintels. *R. F. Mack*

Above Many of the wartime Guy 'Arab' buses were fitted with bodies that used poor quality, badly seasoned wood for their framing. Having replaced many of these 'utility' bodies with pre-war Park Royal bodies transferred from redundant Dennis 'Lances', Walsall purchased new bodies for a batch of ten Guy 'Arabs'. This occurred in 1953 when Willowbrook received the order for these attractive H32/26R bodies. Unusually, they were 7ft 9in wide and all had their springs lowered to reduce their overall height. Numerically the last one of the ten, 215 (JDH 37), had originally been 227 and had entered service with a Park Royal body in 1943. The bus is about to cross the Leamore Lane junction at the Black Horse public house, when running 'light' from Birchills garage, and is being followed by a 1965-registered Land-Rover. *R. F. Mack*

Below The Rosum Cinema in Leamore has succumbed to the delights of bingo by the time Walsall Corporation's 820 (RDH 510) passes it on 11 July 1966 on its way into Walsall. It is working on the 65 service, which was one of the Corporation's longest routes, coming from Stafford in the north to Walsall via Bloxwich, then on to Dudley. The bus was one of the ten Leyland 'Titan' PD2/12s, a newly introduced 27-foot-long chassis, with a Roe full-fronted H33/23R body. They were the first double-deckers in the fleet to be equipped with platform doors; introduced in 1953, they would survive in service for 18 years.

The public house on the right, on the corner of Harden Road, is the Butlers Arms and stands behind its own forecourt, which by the 1980s had become a car park. The impressive bus shelter, which 820 has just left, still stands in silent memory to the long departed trolleybuses. *F. W. York*

Top One of the six-wheeled Park Royal-bodied Sunbeam MS2s of 1940, 320 (HDH 213), turns at the Red Lion/Green Lane junction in Bloxwich Road in about 1953. Its driver is waiting for the four-wheeler to pass on its way of Walsall on the 30 service. This trolleybus is 342 (NDH 959), which was the subject of a major rebuilding that took over seven years to complete, re-entering service in 1967 as a 30-foot-long trolleybus. Both trolleybuses are in the Somerfield-era light blue livery with dark blue bands. The four-wheeler is about to be overtaken by a battery-electric milk float. With its left-foot-operated throttle pedal, a milk float had very similar driving characteristics to a trolleybus, except that of course it was not limited to running where there was overhead. *C. W. Routh*

Middle The north end of Bloxwich Road became High Street at the junction with Green Lane, where the trolleybus turn-back was situated. In about 1965 Walsall Corporation meets Midland Red at Old Lane. The trolleybus heading out of Bloxwich towards Walsall is 854 (TDH 904), which is working beneath the excellently taut overhead on the inner leg of the Blakenall circular service15. The Midland Red is 4114 (THA 114), a BMMO D7 with an MCCW H32/26R body. This bus, one of some 350 D7s built between 1953 and 1957, was later to become the last of the type to remain in service, not withdrawn until 1973. It is working on the 865 service that began in Tipton Road in Dudley, adjacent to the railway station, and went to Stafford by way of Wednesbury, Walsall, Bloxwich and Cannock. The service then connected with Potteries Motor Traction services, which allowed access to the Potteries. Midland Red jointly worked the route with Walsall Corporation, whose buses displayed the 65 service number. *R. F. Mack*

Bottom Having left the Bloxwich shopping centre the trolleybus routes to Leamore and Birchills turned left into the short section of High Street at the Somerfield Road junction near the Parish Church of All Saints. With the Health Centre behind it, Sunbeam F4A trolleybus 854 (TDH 904) begins to make its way down a long, gentle gradient towards the suburb of Leamore, just over half a mile away. It is about to pass the last of the Victorian terraced housing that survived the redevelopment at the Somerfield Road and High Street junction in the early 1960s. The smartly painted Willowbrook-bodied trolley has come from the Mossley Estate via Bloxwich on the 31 service and is being followed by an almost new Austin Cambridge A60, dating from 1964. *R. F. Mack*

Travelling along Bloxwich High Street near St Peters Roman Catholic Church near the corner of Harrison Street is trolleybus 869 (XDH 69). It is passing the new block occupied by F. W. Woolworth as it travels towards Walsall on Saturday 28 March 1970. It appears to be still in fairly good condition, but has had its Walsall Corporation municipal crests painted out.

By this time the 'writing was on the wall' for the town's trolleybus system, and it was being operated by West Midlands PTE. The first stage of the abandonment had been instigated and although this did not involve any loss of routes, many of the older trolleybuses were withdrawn and replaced by former Birmingham Corporation Guy 'Arab' IVs and a few Daimler CVD6s from the PTE's South Division. This Willowbrook-bodied Sunbeam F4A is working on the 33 circular service, but is still displaying Dudley Fields on the destination blind. *J. H. Meredith*

Above Walsall Corporation's last tramcar, 49, was delivered in 1919 and would survive until the closure of the system in 1933. it was a Brush-bodied car mounted on a Brill 21E truck, and is seen here in High Street, Bloxwich, in about 1925, on its way to the terminus, having passed All Saints Parish Church behind the trees. The High Street had developed in the 18th century, and by the early 1920s had become a prosperous shopping centre. In the distance is one of the Walsall's first motorbuses, a single-decker Tilling-Stevens TS3. Between 1915 and 1920 the Corporation bought 17 of these petrol-electric vehicles, all fitted Dodson B28R bodies; none of them would outlast the tram. *D. R. Harvey collection*

Below A Willowbrook-bodied Dennis 'Loline' II, 884 (884 HDH), working on the 1 route from Hednesford, overtakes Sunbeam F4 trolleybus 341 (NDH 958). The latter appears to be in trouble after coming in from Blakenall on the circular 30 service; it has pulled over and is being attended by a number of Transport Department staff. The driver of the Dennis has given the apparently 'dead' trolleybus a distinctly wide berth as he begins the journey back to Walsall. Between the two vehicles can be seen the entrance to Wolverhampton Road, marked by the old-fashioned 'torch' sign to warn motorists of the Church of England school. All the shops on the left, including Groves Dry Cleaners, converted from Victorian houses, have since been replaced by modern purpose-built units. *R. F. Mack*

Trolleybus 850 was Walsall's only post-war six-wheeler and, although 30 feet long, the adventurousness of the concept was not sufficient for the Pay-As-You-Board design to be developed. In 1954 Mr Edgley Cox effectively 'took on' the Ministry of Transport and without the 'official' authorisation of the Construction & Use Regulations, ordered 15 Sunbeam F4As, which were not only also 30 feet long but also had only two axles. This led the way for that length to become available for double-deckers as well as the previously allowed 27-foot length after 1956 for diesel-engined buses. It was ironic that the Walsall trolleybus experiments, first with 850 then with the 22 Sunbeam F4As, could have been a contributory factor in the national demise of the trolleybus! By now renumbered 350, 850 (RDH 990) shows off its rear-end design and, in its rebuilt form, its twin-staircase layout.

The trolleybus coming in to Bloxwich from the terminus is the second 850 (HBE 541), purchased from Cleethorpes Corporation, where it had been 63, one of the pair of Roe-bodied Crossley 'Empire' TDD42/3s acquired new in February 1951. Crossley trolleybuses were a rarity outside their native North West of England, and of the 45 four-wheeled 'Empires' built by the Stockport-based company between 1950 and 1951, the Cleethorpes pair were the only two not ordered by either Manchester or Ashton-under-Lyne Corporations! No 850 entered service with Walsall in February 1961 and was the first trolleybus to operate on the Lower Farm service when it opened on New Year's Eve 1962. It survived into a long period of unloved preservation and, scandalously, was eventually broken up in 1996 after being allowed to deteriorate badly in unprotected open-air storage!

Just visible between the trolleybuses and through the trees that line the High Street is Bloxwich Church of England School. This was originally opened as a National School in 1865 and therefore pre-dates the Forster Elementary Education Act of August 1870. The school was rebuilt in 1878 and the building remains in use today. *C. W. Routh*

Above North of Victoria Street, at the end of the shopping area, Bloxwich's High Street opened out into an area of open space around the Bull's Head public house and Park Road, which has survived through to the present day despite the nearness of Bloxwich Park on the other side of High Street. The Walsall-bound trolleybuses and buses parked on the High Street side of this small area of ornamental gardens. The 32 service from Lower Farm Estate is being operated by Sunbeam F4A 854 (TDH 904); the unusual treatment of the front cab windows of the 1955 Willowbrook body design on these 30-foot-long trolleybuses was regarded as 'unfortunate', giving rise to the epithet of 'Goldfish Bowls'. By way of contrast, the body produced by Northern

Counties, just nine years later and also to the requirements of Mr Edgley Cox, on the short-length Daimler 'Fleetline' CRG6LXs was simply ugly! One of the 1965 batch, 53 (EDH 953C), having come into Bloxwich from Birmingham on the 958 service, has turned around and is 'parked-up' before going back to Walsall and Birmingham.

On the opposite side of the road, behind the rudimentary bus shelters, is what was Bloxwich's Music Hall, built on the corner of High Street and Wolverhampton Road in 1857. Next to it are an attractive couple of contemporary houses, which in recent years have been converted to local government Neighbourhood Offices. *D. R. Harvey collection*

Left A Chase Coaches of Chasetown Leyland 'National' 10351A/2R, 5 (AYR 339T), stands in Bloxwich High Street on Tuesday 9 March 1999. The single-decker is a former Eastbourne Corporation B35D-bodied bus acquired by Chase in November 1990 when it was already 11 years old.

The old Music Hall and the thriving Bloxwich Church of England School in the background are externally, at least, little altered in the 30 years since the trolleybuses last silently glided along the High Street. Although some of the street furniture has altered in this time, much remains the same. Many of the smaller towns of the Black Country have been destroyed by thoughtless redevelopment, but there is a refreshing 'sameness' about Bloxwich that is a result of evolutionary, rather than dynamic, change. *D. R. Harvey*

Above While the original SST steam tram route only went to Bloxwich's Parish Church, upon electrification in 1893 it was extended to the Bell Inn at the northern end of the town. There were originally 12 loops on the single-track Bloxwich line, but after Walsall Corporation acquired the operating rights of all the electric tramways within its boundary from the South Staffordshire Company on 1 January 1904, these were virtually eliminated. The penultimate track alteration on the Bloxwich route took place in last months of 1920 when the whole of the High Street section from All Saints through the shopping centre and on to the terminus was doubled. Tramcar 34 leaves the last of the passing loops and enters a single-track section at Park Road, which dates this photograph to between the end of the Great War and that track realignment.

Car 34, one of the eight open-balconied, vestibuled tramcars constructed by the United Electric Company in 1912 and mounted on Brill 21E trucks, is about to pass Daimler Y-type single-decker 7 (DH 1029), parked on the access road between High Street and Park Road. This bus entered service in 1915 and was fitted with a rear-entrance, 28-seater body built by Willesden-based Christopher Dodson to a design known as the 'Sheffield type'. It is waiting at the original terminus of the service to Hednesford.

After receiving the Royal Assent for the Walsall Corporation Act of 1914, the six Daimler 'Y'-types ordered to operate the Corporation's first bus services to Cannock and Hednesford were impressed by the War Department before they were even delivered. In 1915 Walsall received the first three of a total of nine Daimlers that they managed to purchase from the Coventry-based company during the remainder of the War. The Corporation was fortunate to

retain them, as throughout the country similar chassis, albeit double-deckers, were commandeered by the War Department. Large numbers of these Daimlers and the more famous AEC 'B'-type, mainly from London, were subsequently shipped to France and Belgium to take troops up to the trenches and, like many of the soldiers, were lost in the mud of Flanders. *D. R. Harvey collection*

Above Over 40 years later Guy 'Arab' III 219 (ODH 302) waits at the Fare Stage bus stop in almost the same spot. By now the large grassed area behind the bus, between High Street and Park Road, has been improved by having been formally laid out and given an ornate fountain. The Park Royal-bodied bus is painted in its original, attractive two-tone blue livery and is working on the long 65 service between Stafford and Dudley. It is still quite new as it is adorned with an advertisement proclaiming 'SAY C.W.S. AND SAVE', which appeared on public transport vehicles across the country in about 1952. *C. Carter*

Above Walsall's first second-hand trolleybus purchases were a couple of former Pontypridd UDC Karrier W4s with Roe UH30/26R bodies. This was the first of the pair, which had formerly been Pontypridd's number 14. It came into Walsall service on 1 April 1956 and lasted until 18 February 1962. It is turning off Bloxwich High Street and into the short section of roadway through the ornamental gardens before turning into Park Road. Behind the decorative fountain is the mock-Tudor, half-timbered Bulls Head public house, which had replaced a late-18th-century tavern in 1938.

The Walsall Corporation single-decker that can just be seen standing at the bus stop in Park Road is one of the six Bedford SBOs fitted with Willowbrook B39F bodies that were bought in 1956. Latterly Walsall was never a great

advocate of single-deckers, having only purchased ten underfloor-engined Leyland 'Royal Tiger' PSU1/13s between 1952 and 1953, so it came as something of a surprise when these front-engined, lightweight Bedfords arrived. They were used on the 50 service, which had to negotiate the low railway bridge in Vicarage Road, Pelsall, that ironically would be demolished when the railway line was closed in the 1960s. *S. E. Letts*

Below At the Bloxwich terminus the trolleybuses turned round by means of an anti-clockwise loop in Park Road. This enabled the trolleybuses to face back towards Walsall at the northern end of the High Street opposite Bloxwich Park. Trolleybus 317 (EDH 864), formerly 188, was one of the pair of six-wheeled Sunbeam MS2s fitted with Park Royal H32/28R bodies. It entered service on 28 February 1938 and some 15 years later, in about 1953, waits at this original terminus of the Bloxwich 30 service. Behind it is one of the 1951-delivered Brush-bodied Sunbeam F4s, which at this time were the newest trolleybuses in the fleet. Behind the driver, wearing his winter great-coat, is a Commer Supervan of about 1949, derived from the Hillman Minx Phase III saloon. When new these vans were sold for £350. The Banks's pub on the left is The Bell, on the corner of High Street and Bell Lane, while beneath the M&B Export advertisement on the right is a 'finger' signpost giving directions and mileages to Lichfield, Cannock and Wolverhampton. *A. D. Broughall*

Above Life during the Second World War is frequently portrayed as long, dark days of gloom and austerity. What is forgotten is that generally life went on as normal, the sun continued to shine and the trees continued to grow. On such a day, trolleybus 166 (ADH 12), a Sunbeam MS2 with a Weymann H32/28R body, which had entered service on 10 October 1933, is working on the 30 service back into Walsall, one of the only two trolleybus services operated by the Corporation before the war. The route mileage of 8.94 miles would remain unaltered until the Blakenall route was opened on 6 June 1955. The trolleybus has headlight masks and white black-out edgings, and carries an advertisement for 'Express Powders', an indigestion remedy that would no doubt help 'Connaught Pie' or snook 'go down' better. The trolleybus is standing at the top end of Bloxwich High Street opposite the Bell Hotel. *National Tramway Museum*

Above right During the Second World War certain operators in South East England, specifically Hastings Tramways and Bournemouth, Brighton and Portsmouth Corporations, had a surfeit of trolleybuses as the tourist trade collapsed. Trolleybuses were also more vulnerable in air-raids as damage to the overhead immobilised the system. In the case of Brighton, Hove & District, eight new and unused AEC 661T trolleybuses, which had been delivered in September and October 1939, were stored under canvas covers in Whitehawk Road depot for the duration of the hostilities.

Elsewhere, temporarily redundant trolleybuses were offered to operators whose need for vehicles had increased. One such operator was Walsall Corporation, which received two Bournemouth Corporation trolleybuses in June 1943. These were numbered 78 and 79 in their home-town fleet and had led extremely nomadic lives, having been on loan to London Transport from October 1940 to work on the Ilford service. At the end of this first period of loan in September 1942, they went to Newcastle Corporation. Here, their two-door, two-staircase layout would have been quite normal as this was the standard pre-war practice, considered better for quicker loading and unloading. The pair were then transferred to South Shields Corporation for three months in March 1943 before coming to Walsall, where they stayed until July 1945. Here is 79 (AEL 407) parked, alas not in Walsall, but back in its home town on 15 June 1948, after its return from its wanderings. *A. B. Cross*

Above   Park Road, Bloxwich, was not only used by trolleybuses, but also by motorbuses. One of Walsall's first production, short-length Daimler 'Fleetline' CRG6LXs, 15 (2745 DH), which entered service in August 1964, comes into Bloxwich, probably on a 2 service from Willenhall, although it might alternatively be on a 12! In the distance, in Lichfield Road, is one of the former Ipswich Corporation trolleybuses working on either a 32 Lower Farm Estate service or on the clockwise Blakenall circular 30 service. The

Northern Counties body on the 'Fleetline' is in its original H41/29F configuration; it was rebuilt by Lex Garages in 1971 to have a single, narrow entrance door opposite the driver, as well as the original sliding exit door. If anything could be made to look even uglier, these 25 conversions achieved that aim! *J. H. Taylforth collection*

Below   Standing at the very northern limit of Walsall's trolleybus system is 330 (JDH 430), one of the last wartime-style trolleybuses to enter service with the Corporation, on 1 February 1946, originally numbered 234. It is opposite the Bell Inn public house, Bloxwich, in November 1950, at the junction of Bell Lane and High Street. It was one of the four Sunbeam W4s fitted with a 'relaxed' utility H30/26R body built by Charles Roe, which by this time had a specification that included extra opening saloon windows. Even though it is 1950, Walsall still had only two trolleybus routes, this one, the 30 service to Bloxwich, and the jointly operated 29 route to Willenhall and Wolverhampton. Only with the opening of the Blakenall route on 6 June 1955 did the system began its autumnal-life renaissance. Until the mid-1950s about 34 trolleybuses were in service, but by the end of the decade this had increased to nearer 50 vehicles. *D. R. Harvey collection*

Above The service to the Mossley Estate opened on 3 June 1957, initially only as far as Abbey Square. The route left Bloxwich by way of Wolverhampton Road and joined Bell Lane at Sandbanks opposite the Sir Robert Peel public house. This area of Bloxwich was developed in the early 1960s with a number of 11-storey blocks of flats. Sunbeam F4A trolleybus 871 (XDH 71), working on the 31 service in about 1966, is leaving Bloxwich and is slowing down at the Bell Lane junction to allow a Hillman Minx Series IIIA of about 1960 to speed past. This road junction was closed to through traffic after the trolleybus abandonment, vehicles from the estate then gaining entry to Bell Lane on the other side of the flats. *J. Saunders*

Below The old Sandbanks junction at Bell Lane has been reduced to a wrought-iron gateway into a cul-de-sac leading to the houses on the right, which were built in the 1990s, and to the flats. The only readily identifiable 'sight-marker' from the previous view is, rather strangely in view of all the road realignment that has gone on in the intervening years, the 'Keep Left' bollard and the angled kerb that helped to direct the trolleybuses towards Bloxwich. Travel West Midlands Volvo B6LE 572 (R572 XDA), which entered service in June 1997, speeds out of Bloxwich in Bell Lane when working on the 371E service on 9 March 1999. *D. R. Harvey*

Trolleybus 852 (TDH 902) turns off Bell Lane at the Sir Robert Peel public house when working into Bloxwich on 31 service from Mossley. Sir Robert Peel's father was the Fazeley textile millionaire who built Drayton Manor, near Tamworth, between about 1820 and 1835; today the site is occupied by the Drayton Manor Gardens Pleasure Park. Sir Robert Peel himself became famous for establishing London's police force in 1829, who were immediately given the nickname 'Peelers'. Peel was also the 'founding father' of the modern Conservative Party, which grew out of the Tamworth Manifesto of 1834, and became its first leader. He was twice Prime Minister, in 1834-35 and 1841-46, and died in 1850 at the age of 62. *R. F. Mack*

The pub still prospers today and is adorned by large portraits of the Victorian Prime Minister, making it far less anonymous than in earlier years. One wonders if, in the event of a fracas at the pub, whether the publican would telephone for the Peelers to come to the Sir Robert Peel. Just a thought... The cottages on the corner of Broad Lane have been demolished, while the whole Sandbanks junction has been realigned and widened. In March 1999 a Chase Coaches Leyland 'National' goes past the pub as well as the 'Keep Left' bollards that marked the original position of the right turn into Wolverhampton Road. *D. R. Harvey*

A smart-looking wartime trolleybus, 324 (JDH 331), emerges from Lichfield Road having negotiated the Park Road loop and turns left into Bloxwich High Street. Lichfield Road, by this time the B4155, had been Little Bloxwich Lane, a narrow road that led to the Wyrley & Essington Canal and Little Bloxwich through some of the best agricultural land in the area. The road is today numbered A4124. All the buildings along Lichfield Road have long since been demolished, but those on the corner of Park Road remain today. The trolleybus is one of four Brush-bodied Sunbeam W4s delivered in the summer of 1945 and it is still in the two-tone blue livery. It was renumbered from its original fleet number of 228 in 1950, suggesting that it was photographed in Bloxwich not long after that date. *C. W. Routh*

Above On the last day of trolleybus operation, Saturday 3 October 1970, a special service with a fare of 1 shilling was operated. Twenty years separate this and the previous photograph and in those intervening years the houses on the corner of Lichfield Road have been demolished. Trolleybus 875 (GFU 693), a 1950-built BUT 9611T with a Metro-Vickers 115hp motor, was purchased from Grimsby-Cleethorpes Transport in July 1960, and is working on the 30 route. It had its Northern Coach Builders body rebuilt with a forward entrance and a length of 30 feet, and its seating capacity increased from 56 to 69. Within a month it would be despatched to Wombwell Diesels where it would quickly be reduced to scrap metal. *D. Williams*

Below The trolleybus route from the Lower Farm Estate travelled along Lichfield Road through an area of inter-war, bay-windowed, privately owned housing. This was the penultimate route to open, on 31 December 1962, and had to utilise a lot of second-hand traction poles purchased from other recently closed tram and trolleybus systems. Working from Lower Farm Estate on the 32 route towards Bloxwich is one of the 30-foot-long 'Goldfish Bowls', 852 (TDH 902); it has just passed the Esso petrol station on the corner of Selman's Hill, while to the right is Field Road. The trolleybus wires going into Field Road took the 30 trolleybus service to Blakenall, but there was no facility for trolleybuses to turn left towards Blakenall from the Lower Farm direction. *C. Carter*

Above The crew of the trolleybus prepare their charge for the return journey to Walsall via Bloxwich. The driver consults his running card while the conductor winds back the platform destination blind to show the less than helpful 'WALSALL'. The trolleybus, standing at the Lower Farm Estate terminus in about 1967, is 304 (BDY 808), a 95hp Sunbeam W4 that entered service in September 1947 with Hastings Tramways as fleet number 33, and was acquired by Walsall Corporation in July 1959. The Weymann bodies on these vehicles were perhaps not as robust as was originally hoped and 304 has had all its saloon windows rather unattractively reglazed with white rubber mounts. *C. W. Routh*

Below The terminus of the Lower Farm 32 service left Lichfield Road at Stoney Lane and terminated at the traffic island at the end of Buxton Road, which is behind the parked trolleybus. The Lower Farm Estate had been developed in the early 1960s with a mixture of housing types ranging from maisonette blocks and multi-storey flats to semi-detached and detached houses. The estate had been named after the small 14th-century, half-timbered Lower Farm farmhouse that had been agriculturally productive until the 1950s, before being demolished in 1963. The trolleybus, 864 (TDH 914), was the Sunbeam F4A that had been used on the Portsmouth Corporation system in October 1955 when it was only four months old and still in the first flush of youth. After withdrawal in October 1970, it was bought for preservation and now resides at Sandtoft Trolleybus Museum. *J. Saunders*

Blakenall

The post-war enlargement of the Walsall trolleybus system really began with the opening of the route through Blakenall. Various plans had been proposed to enlarge the original system of the 29 route to Willenhall and later to Wolverhampton and the 30 route to Bloxwich along Bloxwich Road through Leamore. Most disappointing was the failure in 1937 to obtain local authority permission to operate trolleybuses on the Walsall-Darlaston-Wednesbury circular services that were numbered as motorbus services 37 and 38.

The obtaining of the Walsall Corporation (Trolley Vehicles) Order Confirmation Act in 1953 gave Mr Edgley Cox the opportunity to enlarge the trolleybus services into the new housing estates that were developing to the north of the town. The first tangible evidence that the trolleybus system was going to be enlarged was the opening of a new trolleybus garage on 7 October 1954. The first of these new trolleybus extensions took place on 6 June 1955, by which time all of the first 15 of the 30-foot-long, two-axled Sunbeam F4As had been delivered, which enabled the new extensions to be implemented. The new route was the 15 service to Blakenall, which was further extended on 10 October 1955 to Bloxwich, enabling a circular service to be introduced. The clockwise route from Walsall, via Leamore to Bloxwich, then on to Blakenall before returning to Walsall, became the 30 route, and the anti-clockwise service was the enlarged 15 route; frequently, however, blinds were incorrectly set.

The Blakenall service ran through an already established area of owner-occupied and council-built housing to the heart of the area, at Blakenall Heath, where the Early English-styled Christ Church stands behind its stout churchyard wall.

The trolleybuses on both the Blakenall and Lower Farm routes left Bloxwich along Lichfield Road, using the same wiring, until they reached Field Road. The Lower Farm route continued along Lichfield Road for about a quarter of a mile whereas the wiring to the right took the trolleybuses into Field Road and thence to Blakenall.

With a weak sun shining on the recently rained-on road surface, trolleybus 864 (TDH 914) is working on the anti-clockwise 15 circular service from the Blakenall direction towards Bloxwich and is turning on a fairly hard left-lock into the semi-detached-lined Lichfield Road. The Willowbrook bodies on these Sunbeam F4As were undoubtedly built to 'a price', which meant that they lacked twin-skinned interior panelling and had fairly basic interiors. Their frontal appearance was certainly different, even ugly, but they did have electrically operated rear doors, sat 70 people and gave them a comfortable ride, albeit somewhat noisy from the drumming of the body panels and roof. *C. Carter*

Above Willowbrook-bodied Sunbeam F4A 857 (TDH 907) is about to turn left from Field Road into Ingram Road, working on the clockwise circular Blakenall service from Bloxwich by way of Lichfield Road. Tree-lined Field Road is an area of owner-occupied semi-detached housing dating from the mid-1920s. The route was extended from Blakenall Church to Bloxwich, to complete the long circular service from the town centre, on 10 October 1955, some four months after the trolleybuses had been wired up to reach Blakenall. The shortage of trolleybuses meant that it was only possible to operate the full service after the first batch of 15 30-foot-long Sunbeam F4As had all entered service. *R. F. Mack*

Below Passing each other in Ingram Road are trolleybuses 855 (TDH 905) and 337 (NDH 954). The operation of any of the ten Sunbeam F4s built with Brush H30/26R bodies in 1951, such as 337, was not a regular occurrence as their capacity was considered more useful on the more frequent 'main-line' service along Bloxwich Road. This did not preclude them on the Blakenall service, but the newer, larger Sunbeam F4As, as exemplified by 855, were always the regular, even preferred, trolleybuses on this long route. Sunbeam 337 is still in its original attractive light and dark blue livery, while 855 had the Edgley Cox simplified livery, which was all-over light blue with two very thin yellow livery bands beneath the saloon windows. This looked very smart when freshly painted, but as most of the fleet were not perhaps painted as frequently as they might have been, it soon began to fade, looking flat and dowdy. *D. R. Harvey collection*

The tower of Blakenall's Christ Church emerges from the trees in Blakenall Heath off Ingram Road. The church was consecrated in 1872, although the tower itself was not completed for another ten years and is in a slightly different style from the nave. One of the two former Grimsby-Cleethorpes Crossley 'Empire' TDD42/3 trolleybuses, 873 (HBE 542), has been freshly repainted and is looking extremely smart, despite being in unrelieved all-over blue. The Roe-bodied vehicle is working on a National Trolleybus Association tour of the system, which explains why it is carrying passengers yet displaying the destination PRINTE. *L. Mason*

By way of contrast to the new and therefore freshly painted trolleybus in the previous photograph, and as if to prove the point made about the frequency of repaints, a slightly dishevelled 861 (TDH 911), one of the 1955 batch of Sunbeam F4As, stands in Blakenall Heath in about 1965. It is working on the 15 circular service , but appears to be either showing the wrong destination display, or is facing in the wrong direction, prior to using the 'turn-back' loop that would enable it to return in the direction of Walsall. Christ Church, standing behind the trees and the walled churchyard, was built of limestone in an Early English, Gothic-style between 1865 and 1872, when there would have only been the mid-19th-century cottages in the distance. *J. Saunders*

A Travel West Midlands Wright B37F-bodied Volvo B6LE turns from Blakenall Heath beside the walled churchyard on 9 March 1999, the lack of leaves on the trees revealing the tower of Christ Church silhouetted against the sky; today the church is quite splendidly out of place in an area of 1950s domestic architecture. Since the trolleybus was photographed a number of the old buildings have been replaced. The shopping centre of Blakenall, which is behind the single-decker, is disproportionately small in relation to the size of the large housing estate, but suffers from the proximity of Bloxwich's High Street shopping centre. *D. R. Harvey*

After leaving Blakenall Church and running towards Leamore, through a large, well-laid-out former municipal housing estate, the trolleybus service swung to the south towards Coalpool, by way of Harden Road. Trolleybus 854 (TDH 904), one of the Sunbeam F4As so regularly associated with the 15 circular service, climbs the steep hill in Harden Road when working on the 15 route to Blakenall. Behind it is an Austin ½-ton van of the sort that was in production between 1963 and, surprisingly, 1971, outliving by 13 years the Cambridge A55 car on which it was based. The bus is passing the Coalpool Junior and Infants School, on whose wall the woman is resting with her dummied child in its pram. To the left of the trolleybus is the large area of parkland, through which the Wyrley & Essington Canal passes. The Coalpool canal bridge, behind the photographer, has a steep ascent from the east side, as Harden Road climbs naturally out of the valley of the Ford Brook that runs through Rushall. *C. Carter*

Above When it was first new, Sunbeam F4A, the first 30-foot-long double-decker bus of any sort with only two axles, was exhibited at the 1954 Commercial Motor Show at Earls Court on the Sunbeam stand. By the early 1960s this historic vehicle, 851 (TDH 901), had lost its first 'full flush' of youth and had become just 'another' trolleybus in the Walsall fleet. It is passing the Ryecroft Cemetery main gates in Coalpool Lane. The Ford Anglia E494A is no doubt in the second of its three gears as it climbs sedately up the hill, while the trolleybus, with its lightweight Willowbrook body, glides silently by as it descends towards the by now closed former LNWR railway line. *D. R. Harvey collection*

Below Periodically, faults occurred with the overhead, and over the years Walsall Corporation owned a number of tower wagons, some of which were based on converted buses, but others were new as lorries. They were needed in order to reach the wiring, which was usually suspended about 16 feet above the ground. The last of these tower wagons, an AEC 'Mercury', registered TVX 906 in Essex, is parked rather awkwardly in Coalpool Lane; behind it are the bridges over the old railway line. Trolleybus 857 (TDH 857), working on the Blakenall service, inches its way past, leaving the poor electrical linesman to look after himself as the extended trolleybooms pass close by him! Behind the trolleybus is an Austin Cambridge A55 Mark II, of the sort that had its body styled in Turin by the car designers Pininfarina. *R. F. Mack*

Above Occasionally accidents do happen, but occurrences of this magnitude are mercifully rare. In 1949 Park Royal utility-bodied Guy 'Arab' 179 (HDH 943) is attracting a considerable amount of interest having been involved in a major accident resulting in it running off the road in Coalpool Lane and finishing up perilously close to the embankment of the Walsall to Rugeley railway line. The recovery is obviously rather a delicate operation as the angle of the bus is quite severe, necessitating the shoring up the nearside wheels with long pieces of wood to prevent it sliding even further away from the road. It was some considerable time before the bus was winched to safety and recovered.

This was the third of the four Guy 'Arab' Is received by Walsall between late 1942 and mid-1943, and was the only one to be bodied by Park Royal. Unlike later 'utilities' it had upholstered seats, rather than the later uncomfortable wooden-slatted variety, although like all early bodies built to this style the rear window in the upper saloon was panelled over and never glazed. *D. R. Harvey collection*

Below Working along Proffitt Street near Lockie Road is 353 (ADX 191), one of the eight former Ipswich Sunbeam F4s purchased in May 1962. It is working on the circular Blakenall service in about 1964. The older Victorian buildings on the left are close to Stafford Street, which the trolleybus had just left behind. In front of it is the climb up towards the railway bridge, then on towards Ryecroft Cemetery. This bus, originally Ipswich's number 121, was destined to be the last of these Park Royal-bodied 56-seaters to remain in service, surviving until the last day of trolleybus operation in Walsall, 3 October 1970. *R. F. Mack*

Green Lane to Mossley

The main route out of Walsall to the north was the A34 road to Cannock. This was Green Lane, which ran parallel to the Walsall branch of the Wyrley & Essington Canal. Once out of its Victorian inner area, it quickly entered a zone of heavy industry, with large iron and steel works dominating the skyline.

The development of the council-built housing estates in Beechdale, Dudley Fields and Mossley, in the Bloxwich area north and west of Walsall, enabled much sub-standard 19th-century housing to be replaced in the inner part of Walsall. Most of this residential development only began in the early post-war years after the farmland passed out of viable agricultural use at the edge of the existing urban area. Many of the estates are named after farms that had only survived into the first few years of peace because of the need to produce home-grown fresh produce as part of the war effort.

The newly available land was within the existing Walsall boundary, and as soon as funds became available huge areas of what had only recently been farmland were quickly developed. The need for public transport thus became important just at the time when the Corporation's General Manager, R. Edgley Cox, was embarking on

In 1952 the young Elizabeth Taylor and the suave George Sanders starred in the film *Ivanhoe*, which is the current release on the billboards alongside Guy 'Arab' III 6LW 132 (ODH 90), parked in Green Lane alongside the cinema when working on the 1 service to Hednesford. This bus, in its original two-tone blue livery, was one of the 25 Guy 'Arab' IIIs that were fitted with Park Royal full-fronted bodies in 1951; another 25 bodies were delivered at about the same time, but these were placed on Leyland 'Titan' PD2/1 chassis. Other than their respective manufacturers badges, the only 'give-away' difference between them was that the bottom of the front mudguards on the Guys were not flush with the bottom of the front apron, being set back about 2 inches. Behind it in Townend Bank is a 1939 Morris Fourteen, parked in front of the main entrance to the cinema. *R. Hannay*

Speeding towards the town centre in about 1960 is 105 (JDH 259), a 1945 Guy 'Arab' II. The Corporation's new acquisitions during the Second World War were all products from Fallings Park: it had four Guy 'Arab' Is, as the first 500 became known after they were replaced by a modified model known as the 'Arab' II, and an amazing 71 Mark IIs. These were all allocated to Walsall by the Ministry of War Transport between 1942 and 1945, and the Corporation was fortunate to be able to standardise on the products of Guy Motors.

No 105 was one of 36 Park Royal-bodied 'Arab' IIs supplied to Walsall and, unlike many of its fellows in the fleet, managed to retain its original body until it was withdrawn in 1961, just one year after this photograph was taken. It is beneath the wiring that took the trolleybuses to Stephenson Avenue on the A34 main road out of Walsall towards Cannock, Stafford and the north. The cars of the period represent an interesting transition period between the forward-looking models intended to last well into the 1960s and those built in the early post-war years that had struggled through the recently introduced MOT Test. Parked on the 'wrong' side of the road is the 'world's first hatch-back', the Austin A40, with a Hillman Husky beyond it. Following the bus is a former Post Office, London-registered Morris Z-type 5cwt van.
R. F. Mack

his trolleybus expansion scheme of the late 1950s, by which time Dudley Fields and parts of the other estates were completed and occupied.

Not only was the former agricultural land turned over to housing, but in the Leamore Lane area the development of new factory estates also took place in the late 1950s. This has resulted today in a thriving area of warehousing and light industry. Undoubtedly the introduction of trolleybus services into these suburbs to the west of Bloxwich was a significant factor in the extension of the urban area landscape.

Right The last of the 22 Willowbrook-bodied Sunbeam F4As was 872 (XDH 72), which was different from the rest in having a Lockheed braking system. It is travelling out of Walsall along Green Lane having just crossed the Blue Lane West junction when working on the 33 service to the Cavendish Road terminus at Bloxwich Lane. Behind the trolleybus are the multi-storey premises of the West Midlands Police, which have little architectural merit except for the strange winged device on the roof. The Kendrick's eight-wheeler travelling into Walsall is a Foden FG6 lorry, and is passing St Patrick's Catholic Church on the corner of Short Acre Street. *R. F. Mack*

Below Coming into Walsall along Green Lane, just north of the Blue Lane junction, is 70-seater Sunbeam F4A trolleybus 855 (TDH 905); it is working on a 33 service from Cavendish Road and will terminate in Townend Bank opposite the Savoy cinema. Behind the trolleybus is the complex of eight-storey flats that replaced the old Victorian terraces in the area of Algernon Street and Margaret Street in the late 1950s. It was always claimed that roadworks were the bane of trolleybuses, just as it had been for the tramcars that preceded them. Being tied to the overhead, their lack of manoeuvrability meant that they were not always able to negotiate obstructions, but 855 appears to scotch this rumour remarkably well! *R. F. Mack*

Above Once beyond the distant rows of Victorian terraced houses, the character of Green Lane changed dramatically from residential to heavy industry. The road ran parallel to the Birmingham Navigation's Wyrley & Essington Canal, opened in 1797 to serve the local brickworks and ironworks, although it really began to thrive after the Cannock coalfields were developed later in the 19th century. Trolleybus 857 (TDH 907) travels out of Walsall near Rayboulds Bridge and passes some of the smaller industrial premises nestling beneath the cooling towers of the power station. Beyond this site are the large steel tube works that are owned today by Sterling Tube, continuing the tradition of heavy industry in the Green Lane area of Walsall. *D. R. Harvey collection*

Below left The opening of Stephenson Avenue to trolleybus operation took place on 12 September 1955. The service had something of an identity crisis as at first it was numbered 40 and went to Gipsy Lane Estate; this was renamed Beechdale and the service was eventually renumbered 33 with Dudley Fields on the destination blinds. When trolleybuses first ran on this route Stephenson Avenue was largely undeveloped and undoubtedly their introduction served as a catalyst for development. Trolleybus 869 (XDH 69), one of the second batch of seven Willowbrook-bodied 30-foot-long Sunbeam F4As, entered service on 1 September 1956; it is waiting to turn right into Green Lane from Stephenson Avenue when working on the 33 circular service towards the town centre terminus at Townend Bank in about 1960. These seven, together with the first of the second-hand purchases, initially enabled the existing trolleybus frequencies to be increased, then later, by 1959, the routes to Mossley to be introduced, increasing the route mileage to 15.79 miles. *C. Carter*

Right The 33 route displayed different destinations; in this case 855 (TDH 905) is displaying CAVENDISH RD (BLOXWICH LANE). The trolleybus has just crossed Stokes Bridge, which carried Stephenson Avenue over the meandering Wyrley & Essington Canal. It is perhaps a good job, in view of the roadsign, that the trolleybus had not met the cement mixer on the narrow bridge. The surprising fact about the 22 Willowbrook-bodied Sunbeam F4As was that despite their 30-foot length and the driver's unfamiliarity with driving so long a double-decker, they seemed to negotiate all the tightest sections of the trolleybus system quite comfortably. Admittedly, six-wheeled trolleybuses could be of this length, although only the six pre-war

Sunbeam MS2s and the solitary Sunbeam S7 850 (RDH 990) were this long. The only problem was their tendency for heavy steering, irrespective of their manufacturer, which resulted in many 'muscle-pulling' manoeuvres by their drivers. The trolleybus will proceed down the hill before passing Beechdale Primary School and the top end of Cavendish Road. Today this area had completely changed with a large industrial and retail 'park' having been built in recent years. *R. F. Mack*

Below Speeding along Stephenson Avenue on its way towards Walsall is 851 (TDH 901) working on the 33 service, which had been extended into Bloxwich on 1 November 1961, thereby creating another circular service. Parked outside the pub on the extreme left is a Skoda Octavia saloon, manufactured in Czechoslovakia in about

1963. The council-built semi-detached housing lies well back from the roadway and creates an area dominated by the large grass verges. The wide open spaces of Stephenson Avenue, with its long sweeping curves, was well suited to the fast-accelerating trolleybuses, and 851 has pulled away from the bus shelter opposite the Three Men In A Boat public house. This was a reference to one of Walsall's most famous sons, Jerome Klapka Jerome, who in 1889 wrote the book of that name, one of the best humorous novels of the 19th century. Jerome was born on 2 May 1859 in Belsize House on the corner of Bradford Street and Caldmore Road, almost opposite Bradford Place, and was taken away by his parents when he was two years old. He became an Honorary Freeman of the Borough of Walsall in November 1926, but died very soon afterwards early in the following year. *R. F. Mack*

Top The owner of the Ford Prefect 100E, leaning into the rear of the car, is paying scant regard to the approaching trolleybus, Sunbeam F4A 858 (TDH 908), which is working on the 33 service. At the end of Stephenson Avenue were the left and right junctions at Bloxwich Lane. To the left, where the Ford Transit minibus, owned by the Wolverhampton house-building contractors McLean, is travelling, the trolleybuses went into Bloxwich Lane, taking them as far as Cavendish Road. To the right, the wiring took the trolleybuses eventually into Leamore Lane and on to Bloxwich. Opposite the end of Stephenson Avenue is Hatherton County Primary School, which served the educational needs of the local community and was a catchment school for the Frank F. Harrison Comprehensive. *J. Saunders*

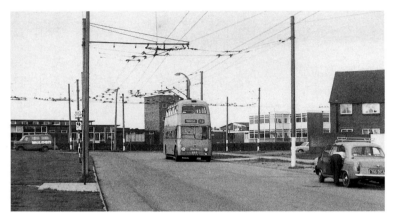

Middle The last extension of the Walsall trolleybus system took place on 2 September 1963, from Stephenson Avenue into Bloxwich Lane away from the rest of the existing route towards Dudley Fields Estate. If the system had been allowed to develop any more, the route would have been extended back along Cavendish Road to form another circular service, rather than pass its eastern end and turn round at its western end. The other option was to extend the service to link with the Wolverhampton service at Bentley, providing a direct Wolverhampton to Bloxwich trolleybus route. The housing estate urgently required an extension of the Stephenson Avenue route, but because of the delays in the decision about the course of the M6 motorway it was put 'on hold' until the motorway's route was fixed 18 months later, signalling the end to further trolleybus developments. Standing in the Bloxwich Lane turning circle at the junction with Cavendish Road is former Ipswich Corporation 120 (ADX 190), now Walsall's 352, waiting to return to the town centre. The destination blind still reads BEECHDALE ESTATE even at this late date, suggesting that these second-hand trolleybuses were equipped with second-hand blinds. Today this site is occupied by the Magic Lantern public house. *D. R. Harvey collection*

Bottom Sunbeam F4A trolleybus 854 (TDH 904) approaches the original 40 terminus as it turns from Leamore Lane into Bloxwich Lane, having returned from Bloxwich on the 33 circular service, which came to this junction at the edge of the Beechdale Housing Estate. The service, originally with the destination blind GIPSY LANE and numbered 40, was opened in September 1955. Behind the trolleybus, in Leamore Lane, are some of the low-rise factory units that characterised that road. Subsequently this area has been renamed the Leamore Enterprise Park, although the buildings have not been upgraded! Except at times of shift changes, this section of the route was less economically viable than the parts of the route that passed through the residential areas. *R. F. Mack*

Right The wide open expanses along the as yet undeveloped Leamore Lane and the parked almost new Hillman Imp car suggest that this photograph was taken in about 1964. The open land on the right would be developed with small production units and distribution and wholesaling centres during the 1970s and 1980s. At the end of Leamore Lane is the Frank F. Harrison Comprehensive, now Community, School, opened in 1966. Many of the schools built in Walsall in the late 1950s and early 1960s, usually identifiable by their flat-roofed architectural style, were named after Walsall Corporation councillors, another example being the T. P. Riley School. Perhaps in retrospect, 40 years on, these educational establishments might have been better named after better-known natives of Walsall; Sister Dora and Jerome K. Jerome come to mind, although perhaps not Richard Wattis or even 'Not now Arthur' Tolcher…!

Sunbeam F4A trolleybus 851 (TDH 901), the first of the 30-foot-long two-axled vehicles, trundles past a new-style school warning sign set alongside the sort of road that seemed to typify trolleybus operation anywhere in the United Kingdom: concrete slabbed and running through open spaces to remote municipal housing estates. *R. F. Mack*

Below The Dudley Fields housing estate was built in the years immediately after the Second World War and had a mixture of mainly council-built semi-detached houses and a few maisonettes built above the local shops. The row of three-storey shops on the corner of Sneyd Hall Road and Central Drive contains Dudley Fields Post Office, which is still located in the same premises at the time of writing.

BTH-powered Sunbeam F4A 869 (XDH 69), with 95hp available through the traction motor, is working its way from the original Dudley Fields terminus towards the town centre on the 33 service. It has accelerated from the shops on the short section of dual carriageway in Sneyd Hall Road and has turned right into Central Drive. Thirty years after the trolleybus abandonment, the traction poles in the Dudley Fields area still remain as street lighting standards.

The outbound pair of wires on the left took the trolleybuses to the other side of the dual carriageway in Sneyd Hall Road in which was located the original terminus. The route is seen in its earlier years of operation, but in later years, as far as trolleybuses were concerned, the words 'Dudley Fields' had more 'grave' connotations. During the 1960s Gammell's scrap dealers was the graveyard for many of the Wolverhampton trolleybus and bus fleet. *C. Carter*

Above The Dudley Fields Estate lies to the south of Sneyd Lane, which links Bloxwich to Wednesfield and Wolverhampton. On the other side is the Mossley Estate, which is built right up to the Walsall-Staffordshire border. Mossley was something of a backwater as far as public transport was concerned, although Dudley Fields did serve as a through route for motor buses from Bloxwich towards Bentley and Short Heath. Working on the 2 service, underneath the trolleybus wires on the short dual carriageway section of Sneyd Hall Road from Bloxwich, is motorbus 123 (ODH 81), a Leyland 'Titan' PD2/1 built in 1951 and fitted with a Park Royal FH30/26R body. The full-fronted design specified by Mr Somerfield might have had some aesthetic merit, but the mechanics at Birchills must have been distinctly unhappy when trying to change engine components in the confines of the bus. The bodies themselves were some of Park Royal's last wooden-framed examples, and by the early 1960s many of them had begun to show signs of 'working' as well as leaking water. The result was that most of those that survived into PTE days, including 123, which lasted until 1971, had been reglazed with rubber-mounted windows; these did nothing for their appearance, but kept the water out! *R. F. Mack*

Below The 31 trolleybus service went to Mossley by way of Wolverhampton Road, Bell Lane and Sneyd Lane. On the left are the roofs of the early post-war pre-fabs, which were by this time at the end of their 'official' 15-year life-span. Sunbeam F4A 852 (TDH 902) has just crossed over the railway bridge near the present-day Bloxwich railway station. This was on the old South Staffordshire line between Walsall and Cannock, which was closed to passengers in BR days under the infamous Beeching Plan of 1963, and the old station was demolished. It has only been under the auspices of Centro that, in 1989, the line was re-opened and a new station halt was built. The trolleybus will continue past the left-hand turn into the Dudley Fields Estate and travel along Sneyd Lane until it reaches Cresswell Avenue, where it will turn right into the Mossley Estate. *D. R. Harvey collection*

Above The junction between Sneyd Hall Road and Sneyd Lane had only a right-hand set of overhead wires out of the housing estates for the 33 circular service to Bloxwich. It was perhaps surprising that it was not therefore possible to take a trolleybus from the Dudley Fields Estate to Mossley Estate. In the last weeks of Walsall's trolleybus operation under the ownership of West Midlands PTE in the autumn of 1970, a number of farewell tours were undertaken by trolleybus enthusiasts' societies. The management of the PTE turned a benign blind-eye to some of the 'unofficial' events that took place on these tours.

Trolleybus 874 (GFU 692), which by now had its Walsall municipal crests painted out, was the only one of the four BUT 9611Ts purchased from Grimsby-Cleethorpes to retained its Northern Coach Builders body in its original H28/26R layout, and here it is doing something 'naughty!' Despite weighing well over 8 tons, it is being pushed by enthusiasts around the non-wired left turn. With its trolleybooms down, two of the 'followers' are carrying trolley retriever poles so that it can be re-united with the power lines to resume its tour. If the vehicle had been fitted with batteries it would have been able to do this manoeuvre without the help of the passengers, but this method of propulsion was more fun! *R. Symons*

Above right The 31 service turned into Cresswell Avenue at virtually the only 'old' group of buildings in Sneyd Lane.

Cresswell Avenue is the main access road into the Mossley Estate, and when the trolleybuses were first introduced on 3 June 1957 they terminated at Abbey Square, which had been built coincidentally as a loop. The Mossley service was soon extended on 20 September 1959 to the Eagle Hotel at the junction with Tintern Crescent. In about 1966, judging by the just visible tail lights of a brand new Vauxhall Viva HB series, Walsall Corporation's trolleybus 854 (TDH 904) turns from Sneyd Lane, with its late-Victorian shops and houses, to start the drive of about three-quarters of a mile to the terminus. The trolleybus appears to be 'packed to the gunwales' with 'Mossleyites' going home. *R. F. Mack*

Above left When the Mossley extension was opened the large space in front of the then newly built Eagle Hotel was used as the new trolleybus turning circle. Beyond Tintern Crescent was a small petrol station on Broad Lane, and beyond that was open land, not destined to be built upon until well after the demise of the trolleybuses. The Eagle was a Butlers house when it was opened, and for many years it stocked Mitchells & Butlers beers rather than the locally brewed Highgate beers. In about 1966 the much rebuilt trolleybus 342 (NDH 959), originally a 26-foot-long Sunbeam F4 with a Brush H30/26R body, is about to leave the Eagle to return to Walsall with its destination blind incorrectly set. In its rebuilt state the trolleybus, which is preserved by the British Trolleybus Society at Sandtoft, looked ungainly with a chassis that seemed too long for its body. Just visible behind is one of the almost less unorthodox of Walsall's trolleybuses, a 'normal' 30-foot-long Sunbeam F4A with a Willowbrook body that actually appeared to fit the chassis. *J. Saunders*

Left On 9 March 1999 Travel West Midlands Volvo B10L 1468 (R468 XDA), one of 80 Wright B43F-bodied single-deckers to appear in the TWM fleet in 1997, stands at the Cresswell Crescent terminus outside the Eagle. Since the deregulation of bus services in October 1986, many new independent operators have emerged. In the Walsall area, the Willenhall-based Midland Choice Travel is one such company, whose fleet colours are bright yellow and green. They both work with and, as at Mossley, compete against Travel West Midlands, using new 'state-of-the-art' single-deckers, such as the Optare XL, R742 BUJ, working on the 171 service, which replicates most of the Walsall-Bloxwich-Mossley trolleybus service. *D. R. Harvey*

Above Standing among the council houses at the New Invention terminus of the 41 service is one of the five unusual Leyland 'Royal Tiger' PSU1/13s that entered service in May 1953. By this date it had been equipped as a One-Man-Operated bus and had a rudimentary sign to that effect on the front panel. These buses were bodied by Park Royal, which at this time was better known for double-deckers. The original order was for 15 Leyland 'Tiger' PS2s, but on his arrival at Walsall Mr Edgley Cox changed the order to ten full-fronted Leyland 'Titan' PD2/12s and these five 'Royal Tigers'. They were 42-seaters but had a fairly lightweight body construction that enabled the all-up unladen weight to be restricted to 7 tons 4 cwt. *L. Mason*

Into the Black Country

Walsall's location at the north-eastern edge of the industrial Black Country in the West Midlands meant that it had to look westwards to maintain its links with the rest of the area. The valley of the River Tame contained numerous other towns, villages and hamlets that during the Industrial Revolution grew to form one large urban area whose local boundaries merged into each other. Today this is part of the West Midlands conurbation, but when mechanical road public transport began at the end of Queen Victoria's reign the individual settlements were fiercely independent and protective of their own industries and cultures.

Initially the local extractive industries supplied the local iron-makers, but gradually the need to 'export' goods meant the early development of canals, in 1769, to link the area to the ever-enlarging Birmingham. While travel along the Tame Valley was relatively easy, the river was a considerable obstacle to traffic travelling across the valley from Walsall to Wednesbury, Darlaston and Wolverhampton. In later years the few river crossing points thus became the main roads, which were followed by the electric tramcars. By way of contrast the valley became a vital routeway in linking the West Midlands to the national railway system that was being developed in the first decade of Queen Victoria's reign. It was on passing through this part of the Black Country that the Queen, who was a notable early traveller on railways, demanded that her Lady-in-Waiting pull down the carriage blind so that she 'did not have to look upon this terrible place'! The Tame Valley's night sky would be lit in a brilliant orange glow from the hundreds of furnaces that were ironically producing the very wealth for the nation that the Monarch did not want to see, but which she presumably enjoyed. In the late 1960s the Tame Valley was chosen as the route of the M6 motorway for precisely the same topographical reasons that had been so important 200 years earlier.

The Black Country is no longer black. The coal, iron ore and limestone were all exhausted years ago and the heavy industry that so characterised the Wednesbury and Darlaston areas gradually became uneconomic. Industry still exists and even thrives in the Black Country today, but the area is no longer beneath a pall of black sooty smoke since the 'greening' of the region began in the 1980s.

Pleck

The development of Pleck, lying to the west of Walsall on the road to Darlaston and Bilston, came in the 19th century when the Earl of Bradford began to exploit the area for its mineral resources. The place-name 'Pleck' originally meant 'a small plot of land', and for many years this area to the west of Walsall consisted of fairly unproductive farmland. By the mid-19th century, with the Birmingham Canal Navigation's Walsall Canal, which opened in 1799, lying to the north and the old South Staffordshire Railway of 1847 to the south, the Victorian terraces along Wednesbury Road were developed. The factories that grew up were iron and steel works, and later gas-tube-making and bedstead and cycle frames became the economic strength of Pleck.

Above Walsall Corporation tramcar 22, a Brush open-topper of 1904 that had been given a 'Magrini'-type short-length top-cover within a few years of the opening of the system, stands in Wednesbury Road, Pleck, before the First World War. It is travelling towards Walsall and is about to leave Prince Street on the right and climb over the railway bridge at Pleck Junction. Most of the properties had been built as houses but had been converted to shops by the turn of the century. On the extreme left, on the corner of Ford Street, is a milliner, reflecting the social mores of the Edwardian period regarding headgear. On the corner of Oxford Street, behind the tram, is the dome of the Hope and Anchor public house. The trams took the Wednesbury Road towards James Bridge at the right fork in the background; Hillary Street, in the distance to the left of the tram, was dominated by the local school. *J. H. Taylforth collection*

Below The main row of shops in Pleck lay along Wednesbury Road from the junction with Hillary Street, to the right of the cyclist, but they ended abruptly where the road began to rise over the railway bridge in the distance at Pleck Junction. On the left is the Hope and Anchor public house on the corner of Oxford Street and on the other side of the road is a tobacconist, whose sunshade reads 'NOTED CIGARS', while beyond that shop is a newsagent with a similar sunshade. Car 27, one of the Brush open-toppers that opened the Corporation system on 1 January 1904, stands outside the public house, especially well loaded on the top deck. It is travelling towards Walsall having come from Darlaston. *Commercial postcard*

Above Travelling towards Pleck in Bescot Road is tramcar 49, a totally enclosed tramcar constructed by the Brush Electrical Company of Loughborough in 1919 and mounted on Brill 21E trucks. It is working from Wednesbury and is approaching the junction with Slaney Road, which is visible beyond the tramcar on the left. Slaney Road got its name from one of the families that occupied the nearby 14th-century Bescot Hall, demolished in 1929 about the time that this photograph was taken. The tram is opposite where today Wallows Road leads off to the Broadway, which was built as a by-pass for the town in the 1920s. Bescot Road was a quiet, tree-lined road with large villa-type housing that dated from the last decade of the 19th century. Although the nearby Pleck Park, the former site of Bescot Hall, has survived today as a quiet haven, since the late 1960s the location behind the photographer is where Bescot Road goes underneath the elevated section of the M6 motorway at Junction 9. *Commercial postcard*

Below The last class of Walsall Corporation tramcars entered service in 1919 and were numbered 40-49; they were built by Brush with totally enclosed vestibules from new. One of the class, Car 43, descends Bescot Road near The Grange on its way to Wednesbury. The distant Sentinel over-type steam lorry climbing the hill from Wood Green and the smock dresses worn by the girls looking into the pram on the right date this photograph to about 1924.

Wood Green was an old settlement that got its name from a 14th-century woodland clearing, and until the 1850s had only been a collection of cottages. The area developed into a prosperous residential area immediately before the turn of the 20th century, and by the time tram 43 was photographed the tram tracks had been doubled on all the Walsall routes, including this one, which was jointly worked by the South Staffordshire Company. The tram route to Wednesbury survived until 1931 when it was replaced by a new fleet of AEC 'Regent' and Dennis 'Lance' motorbuses. *Commercial postcard*

Wednesbury

Wednesbury is one of the oldest settlements in the Tame Valley, dating back to the Anglo-Saxon period, its original name 'Woden's Burg' referring to the Norse God of War. Although the medieval town grew up because of the good-quality farmland nearby, it was originally the local clays that encouraged potters to come to the town and start up small-scale industry. During the 18th century the town really began to develop as an industrial centre; coal, exploited on a small scale throughout the area since the early 14th century, coupled with local supplies of iron ore and limestone, provided the whole of this part of the Tame Valley, focused particularly on Wednesbury, with the opportunity to develop heavy industry. The furnaces of the Black Country had been lit and by 1769 the Wednesbury Old Canal had been built to transport raw materials and heavy goods to Birmingham. The Grand Junction Railway opened as early as 1837 and although none of the towns on the flanks of the valley actually had access to a 'town' station, the links to the rest of the country had been forged.

By the 1840s the town's main industry had become tube-making, which thrived until the Depression. Many heavy engineering factories in the town closed in the 1930s as a result of the 'Slump', but tube manufacturing survived here until the final collapse of the Black Country steel industry in the 1980s. Famous companies such as Russell's Crown Tube Works, the Patent Shaft & Axletree Company and F. H. Lloyds Steelworks all helped to gain the town of Wednesbury its reputation, inscribed in Latin on its coat of arms: 'Arte, Marte, Vigore'.

The town became linked initially to the South Staffordshire Railway in 1850. More significantly, the Birmingham, Wolverhampton & Dudley Railway was opened in 1854; this was the last main line to be constructed with 'broad gauge' track, albeit incorporating standard gauge rails. The line soon became part of the Great Western Railway's line from Wolverhampton and Birmingham to London. This line was closed to passenger traffic in 1972 and the splendid latticed passenger bridge over the railway station was demolished along with all other traces of the line. Today on the site of the old GWR station is the new Midland Metro Light Rapid Transit line station and next to it is the operating headquarters and depot of the Metro system.

Walsall Corporation's tram 23 stands on the railway bridge outside Wood Green station on 27 March 1930 before leaving to go to Pleck. Wood Green was the next station west of Bescot Junction on the former Grand Junction line, which was one of the oldest railways in the country; opened in 1837, it linked Birmingham with the Liverpool & Manchester Railway, famous in 1829 for being the first passenger line in the country. The line ran along the easy gradients of the Tame Valley and the original station on this site, Bescot Bridge, was opened to serve Walsall. When the South Staffordshire Railway opened its line into Walsall in 1847, the station quickly became redundant and was closed in 1850. After the opening of the Pleck Loop and Bescot marshalling yard in 1881, a new station, named Wood Green, was opened here. Tram 23 was originally an open-topper, but was fitted soon after delivery with a 'Magrini'-type top cover. This did not cover the canopies and the tram was further altered by having a dome-roof and its canopies extended over the end balconies, which gave some extra protection to the passengers. *M. J. Somerfield*

Above Oakeswell End doesn't even appear in present-day street maps, but beyond Wood Green, between Walsall Road and Walsall Street, was a narrow stretch of road that lay adjacent to Oakeswell Hall. This had been built in the 15th century and was a half-timbered building with an unusual lantern tower. It had briefly been attacked by the Parliamentary troops in the English Civil War as it was then owned by a Royalist family called Hopkins. It was eventually demolished in 1962. Picking up passengers is South Staffordshire tram 6, which has left Wednesbury and is travelling towards Wood Green. It was one of the 'Tividale'-built trams constructed by the Birmingham & Midland Tramways in 1913 using parts bought in from Brush. To the right is Hydes Lane and Crankhall Lane, which both led to the South Staffordshire Railway line. The tall building beyond the old terraced cottages is a factory that made gas fittings. *D. R. Harvey collection*

Below Inching its way through Wednesbury Market Place on its way from the Holyhead Road terminus towards the five-ways junction in High Street is UEC-built tramcar 34. The policeman on point duty appears to have remarkably little to do except to keep the pedestrians, spilling into the roadway on this busy market day, away from the approaching tram - and the odd cyclist! The tram is leaving behind it the impressive Market Place clock tower erected in 1911 on the site where John Wesley once preached in 1743 and nearly caused a riot. It will take the tram tracks to the left and turn into Walsall Street where it will then turn towards Wood Green and Pleck. *M. J. Somerfield*

One of the South Staffordshire Tramways Company steam trams, probably number 26, a Beyer Peacock locomotive built in 1884, hauls a Falcon-built double-decker trailer through Wednesbury Market Place in about 1890. Wednesbury received its Charter from Queen Anne in 1709, and the bustling Market Place became the centre of the town's commerce, the stalls, both covered and uncovered, bearing testament to the busy trade. The tram is leaving in the direction of Walsall. Missing from this earlier scene is the George V Coronation clock, dedicated in November 1911. The Market Place was characterised by its Georgian buildings which included many shops and the inevitable plethora of inns, such as the Old Golden Cross and the George and Dragon, while the prosperity of the Victorian industry in and around the town produced its inevitable effect on the shape and style of the Market Place. Today it is a designated conservation area. *Sandwell Library*

Above The successors to the Walsall to Wednesbury or Darlaston tram route were the circular 37 and 38 bus routes. The main lay-over stop in Wednesbury was between the Market Place and Holyhead Road in Lower High Street. Leyland 'Titan' PD2/14 823 (TDH 770), equipped with a fluid flywheel and pre-selective transmission, was one of only 11 PD2/14s to be built, Leeds Corporation having the other ten. It had been at the 1954 Commercial Motor Show and had a very early lightweight MCCW 'Orion' H32/28R body, which was given the epithet of 'shivering tin'! Behind

823 is the first Crossley 'Bridgemaster' to be constructed, 825 (YDH 225), which had an attractive Crossley H41/31R body. The buses stopped outside St John's School, with the former Board School opened in 1880 almost alongside the lay-over point. Opposite the buses is the tree-lined churchyard of St John's Church. *M. Norton*

Below At the junction of Holyhead Road and Lower High Street in Wednesbury was a three-way tram junction where routes from West Bromwich to the south, Darlaston and Bilston to the north-west and Walsall to the north all met. The original 1893 South Staffordshire electrified tramcar service terminated here and it was only after 1901 that the triangular permanent way was put in place linking the three routes. One of the original four-wheeled South Staffordshire trams of the 40-55 class stands at the Lower High Street terminus while one of the crew opens the small door in the lower saloon panelling beneath the staircase. Ahead of the tram is the railway bridge over the old South Staffordshire line. This separated the terminus outside Lloyds Bank from St John's Church, with its impressive Gothic spire, described by Pevsner as 'odd in outline'. This impressive church with its contrasting light and dark stonework was demolished in 1985. *Commercial postcard*

Right Between 1924 and 1928 the Lower High Street-Holyhead Road junction at the White Horse public house was unique in the West Midlands as it was possible to see tramcars in service being operated by four different operators. In the foreground in Lower High Street is Walsall Corporation's tramcar 32, one of four UEC four-wheelers built in 1908. It is working on the service to The Bridge in Walsall, which was still being jointly operated by the South Staffordshire (Lessee) Company. On the right, standing at its stub terminus in Holyhead Road, is one of the Wolverhampton District Electric Tramways large open-topped bogie tramcars working on the Darlaston service, which would be withdrawn on 30 November 1928.

On the left, parked at its shelter in the middle of Bridge Street outside the

White Horse, is one of Birmingham Corporation's bogie cars of the 587-636 class. These had been built in 1919-20 by Brush with open verandahs and had been totally enclosed by the Corporation in the late 1920s. Operating from Hockley depot, BCT had taken over the operation of the Birmingham-West Bromwich-Wednesbury service from the South Staffordshire Company on 1 April 1924. Although they were offered the route as far as Darlaston and Bilston, the condition of the track was so poor beyond Wednesbury, and the overhead was side-running, that the Corporation declined. As a result the linking 20 yards of track at this three-way junction fell into disuse and was eventually cut, leaving the three trams to meet at their respective stub termini. *M. J. Somerfield*

Below The trams from West Bromwich terminated outside the White Horse Hotel, in Holyhead Road. After 30 September 1930 the Birmingham trams were left on their own until they were replaced on 1 April 1939 by buses jointly operated on the 75 service by Birmingham City

Transport and West Bromwich Corporation. The White Horse was built in 1846 but was demolished in the early 1990s. Car 514, one of the UEC-bodied four-bay trams originally with open balconies that entered service in 1913 mounted on Mountain & Gibson Burnley bogies, has just unloaded at the shelter on the island at the terminus and is about to leave for Birmingham some 9 miles away. The tram was re-motored in the late 1920s with GEC WT32R 70hp motors, enabling it to reach about 40mph when crossing the Sandwell Valley near The Hawthorns, home of West Bromwich Albion.

It is 25 March 1939 and within a week trams will be only a memory in Wednesbury. Indeed, trams would be finally eradicated from the Black Country in just five weeks, and it was only because of the war that many systems kept going. Just visible behind the tram shelter in Lower High Street, just up from the Midland Bank, is Walsall Corporation Dennis 'Lance' 4 202 (FDH 863), which had entered service in 1938. It has a Park Royal body and is working on the 37 circular service back to its home town. *A. N. H. Glover*

In the early 1960s one of Walsall Corporation's more eccentric vehicles, 401 (YDH 401), stands at the impressive bus shelters in Lower High Street, with New Street disappearing down the hill towards Potters Lane. The bus is a Daimler CVG5; it was fitted, unusually for a post-war Daimler double-decker, with a five-cylinder 7.0-litre Gardner engine rather than the more usual Gardner 6LW unit. The gaunt-looking body was built by Walsall Corporation at Birchills garage using body-frames manufactured by the Oldbury-based Metal Section company. This lightweight bus entered service in November 1956 and lasted into West Midlands PTE days. *D. R. Harvey collection*

The wheel has gone full circle, and trams are back in Wednesbury. The depot of the new Midland Metro is located off Great Western Street, near Potters Lane. This Light Rapid Transit line links Birmingham with Wolverhampton and follows for much of its length the former GWR trackbed. The initial fleet of twin-car articulated units was constructed in Italy, but after their delayed delivery Midland Metro had operational, electrical and engineering problems that plagued Route 1 and prevented the opening of the line on schedule. Looking towards Wolverhampton is Car 05, standing in Wednesbury Station while being used for driver training on 29 January 1999. Behind it is the depot with another one of the 'trams' just visible behind the fence. The line eventually opened for passengers on 31 May 1999. *D. R. Harvey*

Darlaston

Darlaston's industrial growth developed because of the proximity of the famous 30-foot coal seam of the South Staffordshire coalfield. Industry initially took the form of the manufacture of gun-lock firing mechanisms, but Darlaston's real industrial claim to fame was the nut and bolt, invented by Thomas Oliver in 1802. From this humble start grew the large local company of F. W. Cotterill, which later became part of the Guest, Keen & Nettlefold Group of manufacturers of industrial fasteners. The larger company in Darlaston was Rubery Owen, which had been founded in 1893, making components for the cycle, motorcar

and aviation industry and surviving in the town until 1980.

The centre of the town was The Bull Stake at the junction of Walsall Road, Darlaston Road and King Street, where the dubious sport of animal baiting once took place. This usually consisted of a bull or a bear being tied to a large iron ring and attacked by bull-terrier dogs. This took place in this market area throughout the 18th century together with cock-fighting and, later, bare-knuckle boxing until the former was made illegal in 1825. The brutality of these 'sports' rather reflected the appalling lives that most of the industrial workers must have had to endure in towns such as Darlaston.

North of the Bull Stake is St Lawrence's Parish Church, which dates from its last rebuild in 1872, although there was a church on the site in the 13th century. Around the Bull Stake grew a motley collection of shops, but it was not until the construction of the Town Hall of 1888 and the nearby police station that the town's civic pride was really recognised. In the years after the Second World War the heavy industry gradually died and Darlaston was in grave danger of going the same way. It was the redevelopment of the shopping centre in the pedestrianised King Street that began to bring an air of prosperity to the town.

The public transport links to Walsall and Wednesbury were initiated in 1863 by the LNWR's Darlaston branch, but competition from the newly electrified South Staffordshire Tramways route in 1893 led to the closure of the passenger railway. This tramway company had its large headquarters and depot near the town centre off Darlaston Road. Walsall Corporation reached the town on 1 May 1907 and continued operating tramcars until 4 March 1931. The buses that replaced the trams were used on the clockwise 37 and anti-clockwise 38 services linking Walsall to Wednesbury and Darlaston. Although it is now operated by single-deckers the route has survived in a recognisable form until the present day.

James Bridge sounds an important population centre, but it was the point at which Darlaston Road crossed the River Tame. Nearby were the premises of Walker Brothers, which owned the Staffordshire Galvanizing Works, and F. H. Lloyd, which manufactured castings for various railway companies and the Royal Navy. One of the South Staffordshire Company cars, a much rebuilt ER&TCW tramcar of 1901, Car 35, travels away from James Bridge towards Walsall in the early 1920s. It was fitted with a top-cover and the semi-enclosing vestibule screen so that it could work on the Wednesbury-Walsall and Darlaston-Walsall routes as a joint working with Walsall Corporation. Since it was withdrawn in about 1925, this view must date from about two years earlier. The open tourer, registered DH 2685, dates from about 1922 and is being driven by a cloche-hatted woman, who has parked on the wrong side of the road. Coming towards her from the Pleck direction is an early post-First World War Leyland semi-forward-control lorry. Opposite the bay-windowed houses was the South Staffordshire Tramway Company electricity generating station, and beyond that the Walsall Canal, the James Bridge Brick Works and nearby colliery. *Commercial postcard*

Top One of the great curses of the present day is car exhausts, creating atmospheric pollution and accelerating the normal cycle of global climatic and temperature fluctuations. When the electric tram was first introduced it fairly quickly gained the reputation of being an efficient and pollution-free means of transport. In many places it had replaced the fire-breathing, smoke and steam snorting steam trams, whose reputation for many years after their demise was sullied by the protagonists of the electric tramcar. If the Edwardians had gained with the electric tramcar, one thing that they inherited and were to keep for the next 20 years was horse manure, 'pollution' left as tangible evidence of their passing. This can be clearly seen in the roadway as UEC top-covered tramcar 30 stands on a section of single-line track in Walsall Road, Darlaston. *Commercial postcard*

Middle Having descended the hill in Walsall Road beyond Pleck and Fallings Heath, the trams had to stop in the last passing loop before The Bull Stake to see if the track was clear at the terminus. This last loop was at Birmingham Street, whose cobbled entrance can be seen on the right. The public house on the left with the double bay windows still remains today, but the dreadful terraces on the right whose front doors led directly into the front room from the pavement were swept away some years ago. The tram is 24, one of the original cars of 1904, which had received the less than common combination of Magrini-top and vestibuled platforms. It is Saturday 29 March 1930 and the route is in its last 12 months of operation, having still been jointly operated by the South Staffordshire Company only three weeks before. *M. J. Somerfield*

Bottom The Bull Stake at Darlaston is at the junction of Walsall Road and Darlaston Road. To the right and over the LNWR's railway bridge was the headquarters and depot of the South Staffordshire Tramways Company. Standing just beyond the turn into Darlaston Road to the right and the Willenhall line to left is Walsall Corporation tramcar 32, a 1908 UEC top-covered double-decker that was vestibuled in about 1918. It has had its trolleypole placed on the wire for the return journey to Walsall. The wire had a shield over it at this point so that sparks could not be seen at night, remembering the Zeppelin air-raid of 1916. Similar devices would be seen again on British tram and trolleybus systems in the Second World War. *D. R. Harvey collection*

Right On 9 June 1930, just under a year before the abandonment of the tram route, Walsall Corporation tram 34 waits outside the premises of the Midland Bank in the centre of Darlaston in Walsall Road near The Bull Stake. It is waiting for its allotted departure time before leaving for Walsall by way of James Bridge and Pleck; the driver and conductor stand chatting on the front platform as the minutes tick away. The tram is one of the seven top-covered, open-balconied cars bought from the United Electric Company in 1912 and mounted on Brill 21E trucks. They were fitted with platform vestibules from new and at the time were as up to date as any other four-wheeled narrow-gauge double-decker tramcar in the country. By 1 October 1930, only three months away, Walsall Corporation had become the sole operator of trams on the Wednesbury and Darlaston services, having taken over sole operation from the South Staffordshire (Lessee) Company. Their main depot was located in nearby Darlaston Road, but had closed on 31 March 1924. *H. Whitcombe*

Below One of the four UEC-built double-deck trams of 1908, Car 30, stands in Walsall Road, Darlaston, at The Bull Stake. The tram lines can just be seen to take a right turn towards Darlaston Green and the part of the service from which neither the South Staffs Company nor the Corporation was making much profit, the Crescent Road section down to Willenhall. The tramcar, vestibuled from new, waits while its crew pose for the photograph. The buildings in the background would remain well into the post-war era, with the Pearl Assurance sign being a useful landmark. The buildings facing the tramcar have been demolished and a new road built in their place, although off to the left, along Pinfold Street, a number of really old early-19th-century buildings remain, albeit in a parlous state, but worthy of retention and preservation. *N. N. Forbes, courtesy National Tramway Museum*

Above Advertising the locally brewed Highgate Mild Ales is 1938-built Dennis 'Lance' 4 204 (FDH 865), fitted with a Park Royal H28/26R body and equipped with the latest Dennis 'Big Four' O4 diesel engine. Twenty-five of these 'Lance' 4s were delivered to Walsall in 1938. The Dennis is standing near The Bull Stake in Walsall Road, Darlaston, in almost he same position as the tram in the previous picture, near the Midland Bank premises. It is 1950, which would be about one year before 204 was withdrawn and its body transferred to a wartime Guy 'Arab' II of the same type that appears in the next photograph. The Bull Stake was a favoured lay-over for bus crews, as behind the bus was a 'refreshment room' - a cafe where the crews could top up their billy-cans with tea. *R. Marshall*

Below About 20 years after the tramcars were withdrawn, Guy 'Arab' II 44 (JDH 136) stands in Walsall Road at The Bull Stake junction in Darlaston. The Gardner 5LW-powered bus was built in 1944 and was fitted with a Park Royal H30/26R body of the type that were known as 'utilities'. By this time, about 1950, the bus had been equipped with upholstered seats, replacing the original wooden-slatted ones. Other than this, it is in original condition and still only has a pair of opening side windows in each saloon. It is standing outside George Foden's Gents Hairdressers, which, as well as selling Brylcreem hair cream, also seems to sell cigarettes, including the cough-inducing Turf brand as well as other more unmentionable 'gentlemen's weekend requisites'. The headscarfed woman on the extreme left is coming out of King Street, which led into the main shopping area of the town as well as leading towards Darlaston's Town Hall, built in 1888 to commemorate Victoria's Golden Jubilee. *R. Marshall*

The original part of Darlaston depot was converted to electric tramcar operation for the opening of the Bloxwich service on 1 January 1893. The first batch of tramcars were 16 four-wheelers with electrical equipment supplied by the Electric Construction Corporation of Wolverhampton, and 42 is one of the batch numbered 40-47 whose bodies and trucks were built by Brown, Marshall & Company, whereas 49-55 were similarly constructed by the Lancashire Railway Carriage & Wagon Company. Both manufacturer's tramcars were equipped with two 15hp Elwell-Parker DC motors and they had seating for 18 passengers in the lower saloon and 22 outside. These tiny, trail-blazing trams were among the first in the United Kingdom and were destined to have only short lives, so this wonderfully nostalgic photograph must date from the late 1890s.

Car 42 has received some tender loving care with the trucks still being polished by one of the cleaners. The three young lads sitting down have in front of them a pile of old cleaning rags, while at the front of the tram, wearing their official company caps, are the driver and conductor. Trams of this vintage were frequently covered with advertisements for local businesses, in this case Butler's Boots on the upper saloon decency screen, while on the rocker panel the advertisement for the millinery and ladies hosiery sold by Hathaways is beautifully hand-written. *D. R. Harvey collection*

Dudley

The furthest west Walsall Corporation reached by bus was Dudley on the opposite side of the Tame Valley. Dudley, the 'Queen of the Black Country', is different from a lot of the nearby towns, having been built around a hilly defensive site, and even today the town is dominated by the gaunt ruins of Dudley Castle. Every type of mineral resource used in the early days of the Industrial Revolution was extracted in the Dudley area and these hills provided the limestone for the surrounding iron-smelting plants for over 200 years. It was the pioneering work of two local men, 'Dud' Dudley in 1619 and later Abraham Darby at the turn of the 18th century, that led to coke being used to smelt iron ore.

The town was a great influence on the Black Country's development, but it was more surrounded by heavy industry than one of its major centres. Canals arrived in the town in 1779, mainly to carry coal to the glassworks in the Stourbridge area and, after 1792, to transport the limestone from beneath Castle Hill and Wren's Nest Hill to the iron and the later steel foundries to the east of the town in the Tame Valley. Main-line rail links seemed to pass the town by, and although the first line to the town was opened in 1850, Dudley also had the dubious distinction of losing its dingy railway station in 1964.

The ruins of Dudley Castle, the Zoo, which opened in May 1937, and, more recently, the Black Country Living Museum in Tipton Road, have all attracted visitors to the town, and although the effect on the retail outlets in the town centre was pretty devastating when the Merry Hill Shopping Centre was built, the town has begun to claw its way back as an important service centre.

Below The other end of the long 65 bus route, already seen in Bloxwich, was in Dudley. After leaving Walsall the route, jointly operated with Midland Red, went by way of Wednesbury and Tipton to the original terminus in Tipton Road at the junction of Birmingham Road at the bottom of Castle Hill. Here the bus was able to turn around the traffic island opposite the entrance to the Midland Red bus garage. Tipton Road was, in modern-day parlance, an important

Steam trams first reached Dudley in January 1884, when the South Staffordshire Company opened its line from Wednesbury on the 21st of that month. Electric trams first ran here on 3 October 1900, when the Dudley, Stourbridge & District route was opened as far as Sedgley. There was no link with Walsall Corporation until 1949 when a motor bus service between Walsall and Dudley was instigated, and operated as a joint working with Midland Red. This was later extended to Stafford, which made the route one of the longest operated by Walsall Corporation.

transport interchange whose origins could be traced back to the first steam trams. As the bus station was not opened until 1952, a number of Midland Red and the jointly operated Birmingham-West Bromwich Corporation routes also used the Tipton Road island as their terminus.

Parked alongside the advertising hoardings that stood above Dudley railway station, deep in its cutting, in about 1951 is Walsall Corporation 225 (ODH 303), an almost new Guy 'Arab' III fitted with a Gardner 6LW engine and a full-fronted, 56-seater Park Royal body. The roadways at many bus termini were often made of concrete, which was much harder-wearing than the normal asphalt. This resulted in a level, hard standing, rather than the trenched tarmac surface produced by buses always parking in the identical spot in order to load up. The railway station closed on 6 July 1964 as part of Dr Beeching's cuts. *R. F. Mack*

Below left By the mid-1960s the 65 route terminus had been altered from Tipton Road to the top of Birmingham Street, which was beyond the Fisher Street Bus Station opened in October 1952 and much nearer the centre of the town than many other bus services. The gabled ends of Bird Cage Walk opened on 17 April 1964, and behind it the Churchill Shopping Precinct followed the predilection of 1960s town planners to produce a safe, traffic-free yet uninteresting shopping environment. The parked Walsall Corporation bus, 815 (RDH 505), is now preserved at the B&MMOT Bus Museum at Wythall, having survived because of its conversion to a mobile canteen. It is a Leyland 'Titan' PD2/12 with a Roe FH33/23RD body, and entered service in July 1953. It was destined to have a 20-year service life and was one of only three of the ten buses of this type to be repainted in the WMPTE blue and cream livery. *F. W. York*

Off to West Bromwich

West Bromwich was originally little more than a hamlet on a heathland and although it was mentioned in the Domesday Book of 1086 it was only the development of Thomas Telford's turnpike Holyhead Road that encouraged the village to grow. Telford's vision produced what came to be known locally as 'The Golden Mile', stretching from Carters Green in the north almost to the edge of the Sandwell Valley at the Handsworth boundary. This was the long and wide High Street, which soon developed shops, a market and all the civic buildings of the town. The centre of

West Bromwich grew up around the Dartmouth Hotel, named after the Earl of Dartmouth, the local landowner, on the corner of Spon Lane and Paradise Street, which was known as Dartmouth Square. By the turn of the century the length of the High Street was recognisably the same as today.

The best-known of the early manufacturers was George Salter, who made weighing machines, springs and later bayonets, who had set up his works in the 1770s, before the village had started to grow.

With the arrival of the Great Western

The Walsall terminus for the 14 and 54 services was at Bradford Place. Here the buses loaded up outside the Science & Arts Institute, while to their right was the island on which was the town's War Memorial. In this late 1950s view, West Bromwich Daimler CVG6 159 (GEA 159), which entered service in January 1952, is fairly full as the last passenger boards to join the 14 service back to its home town by way of West Bromwich Road and the Fullbrook junction on The Broadway. These attractive-looking buses had Weymann H30/26R bodies and were among some of the last exposed-radiator Daimler CVG6s to be built. By this date the bus has lost its between-deck fleet name due to commercial considerations, and the West Bromwich Corporation fleet name has been placed on the waistrail. Other than that, the splendid dark blue, light blue and deep yellow with black-edged mouldings and gold lining-out contrasted with the all-over 'economic blue' as used on the Walsall Corporation bus fleet. *W. J. Haynes*

The short circular 3 service left Bradford Place and travelled by way of Caldmore Road, Caldmore Green, Milton Street and Palfrey before terminating at Fullbrook. This service was really only a short working of part of the 14 service, which was jointly operated with West Bromwich Corporation. The bus parked in Caldmore Green, pronounced 'Calmer', is a Dennis with a Park Royal H28/24R body, and entered service in 1935. Although it is a 'Lance' II, it has the much neater, earlier style of radiator that was found on the original 'Lance' I model.

Caldmore Green was the centre of a thriving Victorian suburb, which by the mid-

1930s could boast its own cinema, The Forum, while opposite was the large Old Kings Arms on the corner of Corporation Street. As well as these, the area could sport a number of small shops and its own Green, although in this winter scene the greenness was somewhat minimal. Standing outside the County Borough of Walsall police box is a policeman in a high-collared tunic, and propped against the box is his regulation bicycle. The Northampton-registered Standard Flying Fourteen parked at the bus stop – ah, how things have changed – suggests a date of about 1938, although the Morris Isis car behind the bus dates from about 1934. *National Tramway Museum*

Railway in 1854 the town began to expand rapidly, and by1902 electric trams were operating along the High Street. Bus services were first authorised by Parliamentary Act in 1913, but it was only after the First World War that bus routes began to develop. There were two bus routes from Walsall to West Bromwich, which crossed the Tame Valley, one of which, the 14 by way of Fullbrook, was begun on 1 January 1926, while the 54 service via Yew Tree Estate began on 6 October 1947.

Above One of the Park Royal full-front-bodied Leyland 'Titan' PD2/1s of 1951 stands near the Walsall Road aqueduct that carried the Tame Valley Canal over the former Grand Junction Railway line. As the railway was opened in 1837 and the canal in 1844, this is one of the rare places in Britain where the canal was newer than the railway! The bus, 118 (ODH 76), was photographed in the days long before this route across the Tame Valley was made into a dual carriageway and before the valley itself was filled with the elevated M6 motorway. It is working on the 54 service and is facing towards Stone Cross and West Bromwich, having already negotiated the Yew Tree Estate. It is in its original two-tone blue livery and is parked alongside the Navigation Inn's car park, while the wide open spaces of the Tame Valley stretch away into the distance. *D. Williams*

Above right On 6 April 1999 the same spot is almost unrecognisable. The old Navigation Inn had been finally demolished about two years earlier and part of its site has been built on to provide new luxury housing. The Tame Valley Canal is to the right of the single-decker, while the character of Walsall Road, by now numbered the A4031, has been totally altered; it is now a busy dual carriageway and plunges downhill towards the bottom of the valley of the Tame, once dubbed the 'dirtiest river in England'. Also down the hill is the back entrance to Bescot Motive Power Depot and the elevated M6, with its inevitable stationary queue, which seems not only to bisect the Tame Valley but also the whole landscape. Working on the 404 service is Travel West Midlands 1534 (R534 XOB), a Mercedes-Benz 0405N with a Mercedes-Benz B43F body. It is passing Beacon View, which leads to Navigation Lane, beneath the Tame Valley Canal. *D. R. Harvey*

Above Speeding through the Stone Cross area in Walsall Road is one of the Leyland 'Titan' PD2/12s fitted with a Charles Roe body. Its seating layout allowed 33 seats in the upper saloon but only 23 in the lower, which was partly accounted for by the large luggage rack; even so, for a 27-foot-long bus its capacity was distinctly on the low side. It is working on the 14 route not long after it entered service in July 1953. This style of full front had first appeared on 16 similar PD2/12s for East Yorkshire Motor Services, although they were 50-seat coaches. The other ten to be built were these Walsall examples, and once they were in service the design was not repeated, except on an AEC 'Regent' that was bodied much later. The whole of this area to the south of Caldmore had been developed in the period between the wars and the houses behind the bus were from the earliest part of this development. *D. Williams*

Below Approaching the stop at the Stone Cross on its way to West Bromwich is Walsall Corporation's 822 (TDH 769), working on the 54 service that was jointly operated with West Bromwich Corporation. The bus was the second AEC 'Regent' V to be built and entered service in October 1954 after it had appeared at that years Earls Court Commercial Motor Show. It was an MD3RV model fitted with a four-speed synchromesh gearbox and vacuum brakes. The vehicle had a lightweight chassis and the newly introduced AV470 engine was of 7.6 litres capacity. The Park Royal H33/28R body was also lightweight, and although it had an unladen weight of only 6½ tons, the combination of small engine and lightweight body was distinctly on the underpowered side. *D. Williams*

Above Having been given the temporary fleet number 800 in the Walsall Corporation fleet, STF 90, the Leyland 'Lowloader', stands at the Stone Cross public house during 1956. This pub dates from the 1920s, and stands at the junction of Hall Green Road and Walsall Road. The whole area was built up in the 1920s and 1930s with mainly semi-detached housing. The 'Lowloader' is working on the 14 service, which took the direct route between Walsall and West Bromwich, crossing the Tame Valley and reaching the Broadway at the Fullbrook public house. Behind 800 is an unidentified pre-war West Bromwich Corporation Daimler COG6 double-decker, which is turning from Walsall Road into Hall Green Road.

This strange trolleybus-like experimental bus was the first attempt at producing a rear-engined double-decker. Although its Saunders-Roe H37/24R body had an open rear platform, the Leyland 0.350 engine was mounted transversely across the very rear of the bus: its ventilation slats are visible behind the staircase. The bus was demonstrated by Leyland Motors to Walsall for over a year, although the Corporation was a willing participant in the operation of this strange test-bed. *D. Williams*

Right It would be impossible today for a bus to stand outside the Stone Cross facing Walsall as the pub now stands in the middle of a large traffic island, which also includes the old Clifton cinema buildings. The traffic swings through the Stone Cross shopping area with alarming speed yet the small shops have managed to

retain the bustle of an important suburb. The present-day clockwise gyratory system is in many ways the only thing that has changed in the area as the 1920s/'30s houses have remained. This is a far cry from the milepost at the crossroads where the roads from Walsall, West Bromwich and Wednesbury all met at the original stone cross that gave its name to both the pub and the area. For many years this old hostelry, dating back to the time of the Battle of Trafalgar, held locally well-known May Day festivities. Ironically, as far as the pub was concerned, the local Stone Cross Well had what was considered to be the purest water in the area. On a rainy day, 6 April 1999, Travel West Midlands 506 (P506 EJW), a Volvo B6LE bodied by Robert Wright of Ballymena, works on a 403 service on its way back to West Bromwich. *D. R. Harvey*

Above Walsall Corporation bought quite a large number of single-deckers before the Second World War because of the number of routes that had to clear the numerous low bridges in their operating area. One such route was the service between West Bromwich and Aldridge. On 10 April 1949 Dennis 'Lancet' II 88 (FDH 704), a Park Royal-bodied 38-seater, stands outside Burton's gentlemen's outfitters in West Bromwich High Street. One of a batch of ten 'Lancets' delivered in 1938, 88 would remain in service until Coronation year. Behind the bus are passengers waiting for the next 220 service to Bearwood via Rolfe Street. One of the features of High Streets up and down the country about this time was the use of pull-down sun-blinds, which, like women wearing hats, everyone smoking cigarettes and cars backfiring, seems to have faded away into another age. *R. Marshall*

Below Working along West Bromwich High Street on the way out of town on the 14 service back to Walsall by way of Stone Cross is nearly new double-decker 833 (WDH 908), a Daimler CVG6 with a low-build Willowbrook H37/29R body that entered service in March 1956. Overtaking it is a Bedford CA van, with a split windscreen and sliding doors that seemed to either slam open or closed at the least provocation. Behind the bus is a Bedford PC van from another generation, in this case dating from about 1947. The bus is passing two well-known shops that are now a distant memory; A. D. Wimbush, the Small Heath bakery, still exists in the form of the Three Cooks Bakery, but the outfitters Weaver to Wearer has long since disappeared. *D. Williams*

Above The last front-engined buses bought by Walsall Corporation were 15 forward-entrance Daimler CVG6s, with 65-seater bodies built by Metro-Cammell. They arrived in the spring of 1963 and within 18 months the next batch of buses to arrive were the Edgley Cox specification short-length Daimler 'Fleetlines'. Most of these Daimlers were to remain in service until about 1976-77, and in fact outlived some of the first 'Fleetlines'. Daimler 71 (771 UDH) has turned from Paradise Street into Queen Street and is approaching the terminus. Behind it, working on the 6 service to Hamstead, is one of West Bromwich Corporation's 30-foot-long Daimler CVG6/30s, which were also bodied by Metro-Cammell, although in this case they were rear-entrance 73-seaters. The whole of this central area of West Bromwich has now been extensively redeveloped and is part of the pedestrianised High Street scheme. *A. Yates*

Below The 14 and 54 terminus at the West Bromwich end of the journey was altered from Paradise Street to Queen Street on 20 September 1954. This was opposite the Kings cinema in Paradise Street, in the background, which appears to be offering a less than cultural form of light entertainment. This service shared the street as a terminus with the Midland Red routes 220 and 221 to Bearwood, which were, like the 14 and 54, operated in conjunction with West Bromwich Corporation. 'Easy-drive' Leyland 'Titan' PD2/14 823 (TDH 770) waits for another load of passengers to fill its already well-steamed-up Metro-Cammell lightweight 'Orion' body before returning via the Fullbrook Estate to the Bradford Place terminus in Walsall. The building with the canopy on the right contains the offices of the Refuge Assurance Company. *D. Williams*

Out to Walsall Wood and Lichfield

The first tramcar service to the north-east of Walsall was opened by the South Staffordshire Company on 1 January 1893 and went along Lichfield Street and, after passing the then recently opened Arboretum, terminated at Mellish Road. The extension of the electric tram service to Rushall and Walsall Wood, 3½ miles away, might have been something of a surprise as it did not pass through an industrial landscape; in fact the whole area was largely open farmland.

The first bus services to the north of Walsall on the edge of Cannock Chase were operated by the London & North Western Railway, which had opened two double-deck bus services, using a pair of Milnes-Daimlers and two later Commers, between Brownhills and Hednesford in late 1912 and June 1913, but the effects of the First World War meant that they were closed along with most of the LNWR bus services on 17 April 1915. Meanwhile, Walsall Corporation began to operate in May 1915 its first motor bus service, which was operated from Bloxwich to Cannock and Hednesford, giving the Corporation its first foothold in the South Staffordshire area. Agreements were drawn up immediately after the First World War with the Birmingham & Midland Motor Omnibus Company to establish the Corporation's operating territory over which the company would not encroach.

By the end of the 1920s motor bus services were greatly expanded outside the municipal boundaries and across areas that were either only served by railways carrying only minerals from the Cannock Chase coalfield or on routes between the towns lying to the north and east of Walsall that the local BET operator had considered to be uneconomic. About this time Walsall Corporation was turning to the abandonment of its tram services and was introducing a small fleet of motorbuses.

The first tram route to be withdrawn was that to Walsall Wood, on 31 March 1928, which had been losing money for years, and the opportunity was quickly taken to continue a bus route from Walsall Wood to Lichfield. The LNWR's successor, the LMS, was at about this time divesting itself of its ever enlarging bus fleet, as was the GWR and the LNER, and taking up shares in the local BET companies, in this case the Birmingham & Midland Omnibus Company. As many of these routes had not been previously operated or competed for, the services introduced to Brownhills and Lichfield were not objected to by any of the other possible large bus operators. Walsall Corporation and, in slightly different circumstances, Wolverhampton Corporation both managed to retain their original operating rights because of the terms of their respective operating Acts of Parliament. The Walsall Corporation Act of 1914 and subsequent acts enabled Walsall Corporation to operate vehicles outside its boundary, with the result that the area to the immediate south and east of Cannock Chase became an important operational area for the Corporation. Later, in 1944, the Cannock to Lichfield service, which became Walsall's 44 route, was taken over from Sanders of Chasetown. By the early post-war years Walsall Corporation buses were operating intensive services throughout the area between Walsall, Brownhills and Lichfield.

Above Climbing up the hill from the entrance to the Arboretum in Lichfield Street are two Walsall Corporation buses. The leading vehicle, on the 48 service to High Heath, is heavily rebuilt Park Royal-bodied Guy 'Arab' III 183 (ODH 100), whose somewhat flimsy composite-construction Southall-built body was considerably modified in the mid-1960s with the fitting of rubber-mounted saloon windows. It entered service with Walsall Corporation in February 1951 and survived into West Midlands PTE ownership to make it into its 20th year of service. It is being followed by a 30-foot-long Daimler CVG6/30 with a Metro-Cammell 72-seater forward-entrance body, which entered service in July 1961. This bus is working on the 36 service to Castlefort Estate, Walsall Wood. *R. H. G. Simpson*

Below Also climbing Lichfield Street from the junction with Littleton Street is one of Walsall Corporation's forward-entrance, Willowbrook-bodied Dennis 'Loline' II YF2s, 881 (HDH 881), working in the 23 service to Brownhills. Walsall Arboretum, on the left, first opened on 2 May 1874. It was on land, formerly a flooded limestone working, leased for 99 years from Lord Hatherton. After years of losing money, the Arboretum was bought by the Corporation for £4,600 and was finally opened as a free public park on 21 July 1884. Today it is one of Walsall's treasures, with a large variety of species of trees in mature groves and stands. Every year it hosts the famous Walsall Illuminations, first organised on 15 September 1951, which rank only second in size and brilliance to those on the Promenade at Blackpool. *D. Williams*

Top Travelling down the hill in Lichfield Street, with the Arboretum on the left, is open-topped, Brush-built, 48-seater tram 27. Within a few years of entering service this tramcar would be fitted with a flat-canopied, open-balconied top-deck, which would transform its appearance. It is working on the Walsall Wood route, an extension of the original South Staffordshire electric tram service that was opened after the take-over of the route by the Corporation on New Year's Day 1904. The extension only went as far as Mellish Road, which marked the northern edge of the Arboretum and was laid out in 1869, named after the family that occupied the Rushall Hall Estate. The tram is standing in one of the original passing loops in Lichfield Street at Butts Road, and the picture dates from about 1905, as the track has not been doubled. *D. R. Harvey collection*

Middle The main obstruction on the route to Rushall and Walsall Wood was the Rushall Navvies railway bridge carrying the Midland Railway's Walsall to Water Orton line over Lichfield Road; it had distinctly limited headroom for double-decker top-covered tramcars. About to pass underneath the bridge, advertising 'Worthington Ales', is tram 24, one of the Corporation's original open-toppers that had been fitted with a Magrini-type top, characterised by having an enclosed upper saloon, but without canopies over the balconies. It is Saturday 31 March 1928, the last day of tramcar operation to Walsall Wood. The following week brand-new Dennis H double-deckers would take over the operation of the route. *D. R. Harvey collection*

Bottom The terminus of the Walsall Wood tram route was 3½ miles away from its town terminus at The Bridge. The trams faced a long climb from Shelfield to Walsall Wood High Street, and the steepness of this hill can be seen behind the tram. The route terminated at the junction with Coppice Road, where the horse and cart and the little girl are standing. Behind the girl are the trees of St John's Church, whose tower and chancel date from 1837, the same year as the accession of Princess Victoria. Many of the houses along the High Street have been converted into small shops, and corner sites became the most sought after as they gave the premises two windows in which to display wares. On the extreme left, on the corner of Beechtree Road, is one such shop, although Emery's trade as a hatter would today be regarded as unusual. The shops in the High Street appear to have nearly taken over every house and a number of them have their sunshades pulled down.

Tram 25, originally opened-topped, was fitted with a Milnes-Voss totally enclosed top-deck within a year of entering service and its clerestory lights can be seen through the upper deck windows. It was vestibuled midway through the First World War, suggesting that this photograph was posed for by its driver and conductor in about 1910. *A. D. Packer collection*

Above The 16 service to Lichfield left Walsall by way of Rushall and Walsall Wood. Walsall Corporation double-decker 232 (ODH 309), a 1951 Guy 'Arab' III 6LW with a Park Royal FH30/26R body, has climbed up Lichfield Road to reach the Shire Oak junction at Chester Road on its way into Walsall. In crossing this important road junction the bus was also about to cross the boundary from Staffordshire into the West Midlands conurbation. The bus is ticking over with the inevitable Leyland 0.600 engine's shiver as it waits for the traffic lights to change. Passengers found this apparently isolated spot a useful stopping-off point on the 16 route as, just over half a mile away to the left, was the small shopping centre in High Street, Brownhills. *D. Williams*

Below On a misty morning Leyland 'Titan' PD2/1 239 (ODH 811), which entered service in October 1951, pulls away from the two passengers it has just dropped off and continues the climb up to the traffic lights at the Shire Oak. It was here that the route crossed the A452 Chester Road. The bus is travelling towards Walsall and is working on the 16 service. Judging by the amount of body-sag on its Park Royal FH30/26R body, the vehicle is not in 'rude health' and will be extensively rebuilt to extend its life for another seven or so years. These powerful Leyland buses, with their 9.8-litre engines, were ideal for these long, almost inter-urban services operated by the Corporation. It was such a shame that Walsall's financial stringency demanded that its ordered bus bodies were frequently at the cheap end of the market. *R. F. Mack*

Above Working on the 47 service between Walsall, Lichfield and Cannock in 1961 is an almost new, advert-free AEC 'Regent' V 2D2RA, with a Metro-Cammell H41/31F body. These semi-automatic 'Mono-Control' 'Regents' had pleasantly sophisticated chassis and it was a shame that they suffered from having the lowest specification of MCCW 'Orion' body. They were among the last 30-foot-long, half-cab buses bought by the Corporation earlier in the same summer. Standing in The Friary, Lichfield, is 893 (893 MDH); the bus station was off Birmingham Road, some of whose shops are in the background. These appear to be closed, suggesting that the photograph was taken on a Sunday. Visible behind the hedge is a Midland Red underfloor-engined single-decker, which is advertising Dudley Zoo. *R. F. Mack*

Below Lichfield's new bus station is situated in Birmingham Road opposite Lichfield City railway station, and has a much larger capacity, as well as the advantage of shelters that could not be questioned under the terms of the Trade Descriptions Act. Short-length Daimler 'Fleetline' CRG6LW 29 (BDH 429C), which had a Northern Counties H41/29F body and entered service in January 1965, has arrived after working on the 16 service, which gained the city from Walsall by way of Muckley Corner, where the A5 intersects the A461 road from Walsall Wood. After six years in service, in 1971, the bus was rebuilt with a single-door, rather thin front entrance to augment the original large sliding central door. *R. Weaver*

Around the Chase: Cannock and Hednesford

The town of Cannock developed as the focus of the important Cannock Chase coal-mining industry during the Victorian period. Although some of the earlier pre-industrial Georgian buildings survived beyond the Second World War, the redevelopment of the 1960s took away a lot of the older buildings after years of neglect. More recently, the whole area around the A5, Watling Street, has been re-landscaped after many years of dilapidation and its character has been totally transformed since the end of the 1960s. Nearby is Hednesford, which for many years consisted of miners'

Right The original 22 service was operated by Walsall Corporation between Heath Hayes, Cannock and Cheslyn Hay. The conductor of the single-decker has just completed changing the destination blind, no doubt his energetic clamberings amusing the driver whose generosity of spirit had not gone so far as to get out of the cab and do it himself! The bus, 134 (DDH 801), a 1937 Dennis 'Lancet' II fitted with a Park Royal B38F body, is waiting at Heath Hayes in August 1954 before returning to Cheslyn Hay. The four-cylinder Dennis O4 6.5-litre engine had the advantage of being extremely compact, allowing the front bulkhead to be further forward than on many other single-deck chassis built in the late 1930s. The result was that the 'Lancet' II had the potential for a higher than normal seating capacity, which locally was only matched by Midland Red's SOS SON single-deckers. *R. Knibbs*

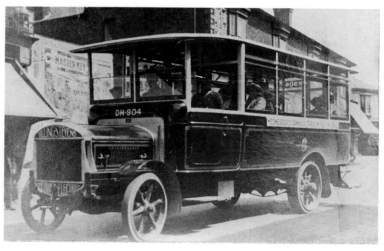

Right Still fairly new, one of the Tilling-Stevens TS3s built in 1915, 4 (DH 904), waits in Market Street, Hednesford High Street, about to work on the service back to Walsall by way of Cannock and Great Wyrley. This Dodson-bodied bus had petrol-electric transmission, which was considered by the War Department to be too complicated to maintain. This resulted in the Tilling-Stevens TS-type chassis not being commandeered by the WD for troop transport use in Flanders. Walsall received six of these buses during the First World War and DH 904 was the first of a pair introduced in the year of the First Battle of Ypres, the sinking of the *Lusitania* and Gallipoli. By being able to purchase the Tilling-Stevens chassis, Walsall was able to expand its services into the Cannock Chase area, to the north and north-east of Bloxwich, before any other operator could gain a toe-hold, once the LNWR had given up bus operation with their ancient Milnes-Daimler and Commer double-deckers. *D. R. Harvey collection*

terraces, coal pits and spoil heaps, while Burntwood was also an important colliery town.

The bus services operated in this coal-mining area around Cannock, Hednesford, Heath Hayes and Burntwood had been mainly provided since the middle of the 1920s by Walsall Corporation. As well as having outposts to Rugeley and Stafford, they also operated works services to many of the numerous collieries in the area. Other local stage carriage and works services were run by Whieldon's Green Bus Company of Rugeley, Churchbridge Luxury Coaches of Cannock and, from the east of the area, by Harper Brothers of Heath Hayes.

Above The bleak open spaces of Hednesford Bus Station look distinctly uninviting on a rainy Staffordshire day. It is situated off Victoria Street, and by 1965 the adjacent railway station had been closed and the line reduced to freight-only working; it has since been re-opened by Centro through to Stafford. Advertising the delicious, but alas defunct, Fillerys Toffees, a bedraggled 822 (TDH 769) waits to work on the short 8 service back to Cannock. This bus was the second AEC 'Regent' V to be constructed and was fitted with a Park Royal body whose design, at the rear end, had a certain similarity to the London Transport RT. The identity of the large parked three-light car of the immediate pre-war period on the right is the main mystery in this photograph. At first sight it looks like an Austin Ranelagh Twenty-Eight, except that the rake of the windscreen is too great. *A. J. Douglas*

Opposite above Walsall Corporation ran a large number of colliery services in the Cannock Chase and Great Wyrley areas, and although never very remunerative, they at least provided a regular income for the Corporation as its 'bread and butter' work. The 115 service was one of these, running from Walsall to Bloxwich, then on to the Wyrley No 3 colliery. Standing among the colliery buildings in a black,

wet landscape is the prototype Dennis 'Loline' Mk II, 885 (885 LDH). This forward-entrance Willowbrook-bodied bus had been an exhibit at the 1960 Commercial Motor Show and differed from the rest of Walsall's 'Lolines' by having rear-axle air suspension. *L. Mason*

Opposite below Standing in the centre of Cannock in about 1957, before many of the old buildings were swept away in the anonymous redevelopment that affected the town in the 1960s, are two sparkling Walsall Corporation buses. The leading vehicle is 232 (ODH 309), a 1951 Guy 'Arab' III 6LW with a full-fronted Park Royal H30/26R body. It is working on the 7 service to Hednesford via Pye Green, suggesting that the destination display of 'Rawnsley' might be incorrect. When new, these buses were kept in excellent condition; although 232 has recently received the simplified all-blue livery, relieved with three of the thinnest yellow bands imaginable, it is very smart. In later years the composite-construction Park Royal body would show distinct signs of wear and tear over the indifferent road surfaces of the Corporation's operating area, and this bus would be withdrawn quite early, in 1967.

Behind it is one of the splendid Roe-bodied Leyland

'Titan' PD2/12s built in the summer of 1953. This bus is working on the 39 Cannock Circular service via Limepit Lane, which was operated jointly with Midland Red.

About to overtake the two buses is a 1957 Vauxhall Victor F-model. This was the first medium-sized saloon car to have an American-styled 'wrap-round' windscreen, the first Vauxhall not to have the famous bonnet flutes, and the first car to have the dubious styling honour of having its exhaust-pipe emerging through the rear bumper over-riders. They were also well-known as being 'rust-buckets'! *R. F. Mack*

Above Passing along the main A34 through the middle of Cannock on 19 April 1962 is one of the five former London Transport RTLs that were purchased by Mr Edgley Cox in 1959 when some became surplus to requirements in the capital. Formerly LTE's RTL 1492, Walsall Corporation's 204 (OLD 601), a Park Royal-bodied Leyland, was a real bargain as it was new on April 1954 and was therefore only five years old when it was purchased. It is working on the 7 service to Cheslyn Hay and has just passed Taylor's cake shop, which was one of the confectionery delights of Cannock at that time. Although still carrying its rear-wheel hub-cap discs, 204 has already been 'tinkered with' as the original destination boxes have been blanked out and a rather home-made single-aperture substituted for the destination. The nearby independent operator, Harper Brothers of Heath Hayes, also operated similar former London Transport buses and they too were similarly modified. The bus is being followed by a Ford

Consul Mark II 204E, which could be distinguished from the slightly later model by its higher domed roof-line. *J. Cockshot*

Below Standing in the centre of Cannock, beneath the trees alongside the large 14th-century Parish Church of St Luke's, is brand new 896 (896 MDH), one of the five Willowbrook 72-seater AEC 'Regent' V 2D2RAs that entered service in 1961. They were numerically the last 30-foot-long half-cab, front-engined double-deckers to enter service with Walsall Corporation, and 896 is working on the Cannock and Limepit Lane Circular service. About to overtake the bus is a Commer Superpoise Super Capacity van, which was more usually known simply as the 30cwt. This belongs to Taylors, the local baker that had retail outlets in the town and surrounding area. On the left is a Thames 15cwt van, which was in production from 1958 until 1965, when it was replaced by the ubiquitous Ford Transit. *R. F. Mack*

Above Perhaps the most significant bus bought by Walsall Corporation after the trail-blazing 30-foot-long Sunbeam F4A trolleybuses of 1955 was the bus exhibited at the 1962 Commercial Motor Show. This was 1 (1 UDH), which entered service in November of that year and was the prototype short-length Daimler 'Fleetline' CRG6LX that had a Northern Counties centre-entrance body. With experience of operation, it proved to be too short and cramped at 25ft 7in, but was still a revolutionary vehicle. It is leaving the concrete bus shelter in Stafford Road Bus Station on the 47 service to Lichfield via Burntwood, Heath Hayes and Cannock. Parked behind it is Green Bus of Rugeley's 26 (DXD 42C), an AEC 'Reliance' 2U3RA with a Plaxton 'Highway' B61F body; this contained only four fewer seats than the short-length Daimler 'Fleetline'. *A. J. Douglas*

Below Well over half the services operated by Walsall Corporation were outside the town's boundaries. This vast operating area extended not only into the Black Country but also into the area to the north and east of the town. Here 848 (248 HDH), a 1960 Dennis 'Loline' II YF2 with a Willowbrook H44/30F body, loads up in Cannock Bus Station at the typical early post-war concrete and glass bus shelters in about 1965. It is being overtaken by one of Green Bus of Rugeley's Guy 'Arab' IIs. This bus, 37 (DTR 921), was purchased in January 1964 from Southampton Corporation where it had been number 98. It was one of the last 'Arab' IIs to be built, entering service in 1948, and had a Park Royal H30/26R body that was very similar to those registered MDH in the Walsall Corporation fleet. *R. F. Mack*

Above The terminus of the long 65 service in Stafford was next to the cattle market near Stafford's large railway station. Working on this route in 1950 is Walsall's Park Royal-bodied Guy 'Arab' III 5LW 98 (MDH 314), a 56-seater dating from 1948 and still in the two-tone blue livery. Parked behind it are two Midland Red SOS FEDDs, both belonging to the long-lived BHA-registered batch of 135 Metro-Cammell-bodied examples that entered service in 1935 and 1936. The slat-sided wagon on the right, which is obstructing part of the bus station, appears at first sight to be a cattle wagon, but where are the cattle or the even the straw animal bedding, and why is it apparently carrying furniture? *A. B. Cross*

Left Passing Greatrex's coach station in Lichfield Road is a Walsall Corporation wartime Guy 'Arab' II (JDH 265). This was one of Walsall's 'utility' double-decker that were not rebodied, and is still fitted with its original Park Royal body. It is off-service and off-route as it is being used on a learner duty, and is overtaking a locally registered Wolseley 1500 of 1961. This was a British Motor Corporation car and was based on Morris Minor running units; the similar Riley 1.5 had much better performance, but less interior polished wood! The old-established Stafford-based coach company of Greatrex is advertising holiday express services to such seaside resorts as Skegness, Blackpool, Colwyn Bay and Lowestoft. Coaches were a cheap way to get to the seven-days bed-and-breakfast holiday, which at this time was unaffected by the imminent boom in cheap overseas package holidays. *S. E. Letts*

Trolleys to Wolverhampton

Of all the UK's 50 trolleybus systems, there were only eight examples of joint operation, the others being Ashton-under-Lyne and Oldham Corporations, Ashton, again, and Manchester Corporation, Brighton Corporation and Brighton, Hove & District, Grimsby Corporation and Cleethorpes Corporation, Mexborough & Swinton, a BET company, and Rotherham Corporation, Nottingham Corporation and the Nottinghamshire & Derbyshire Traction Company, and South Lancashire Transport and St Helens Corporation.

The notable joint operation in the West Midlands was the 29 service between Walsall and Wolverhampton via Bentley and Willenhall. Wolverhampton Corporation had opened the trolleybus service on 16 September 1927 as far as Willenhall, which marked the limit of Wolverhampton's operational boundary. After the failure to agree with the adjacent Corporation about the extension of the new trolleybus service into Walsall, a jointly operated single-deck motorbus service began on 4 February 1929. This was the day after Walsall Corporation had closed its tram route to Willenhall. Walsall was reluctant to invest in the infrastructure required for trolleybus operation. It had been agreed that if the receipts warranted it, Walsall would convert the route to trolleybus operation, providing that the road beneath a low canal bridge in Horseley Fields was lowered to enable double-deckers to pass through. This was completed in mid-September 1930 and the joint working of double-deck trolleybuses began on Monday 16 November 1931.

The route, by now numbered 29, was left unaltered until Wolverhampton took the decision to begin to close down its trolleybus system. By the early 1960s the pendulum had swung totally the other way, and it was at the insistence of Walsall Corporation that the joint service remain operated by trolleybuses until at least 1967. However, the national needs for a motorway linking the Midlands and the North West rather overtook the fortunes of a solitary trolleybus route and after much wrangling over the proposed route, construction of the new motorway began in 1963. It cut across the trolleybus route at Bentley, destroying Bentley Hall at the same time. Eventually construction restrictions became so bad that the trolleybus service closed on 31 October 1965 (see page 160).

In the early years of the service the Walsall end of the 29 route used the large open area at the top of Townend Bank outside Her Majesty's Theatre to turn round. Here we see the inaugural Walsall trolleybus, 151 (DH 8313), which entered service on 22 July 1931 when the town's first trolleybus service opened as far as Willenhall. This was the first of a pair of AEC 663Ts with English Electric H32/28R bodies. It has come out of Wolverhampton Street in about 1936, which would be not too long before the old Victorian theatre was pulled down. The trolleybus body was unusual because the opening windows in the upper saloon were full-opening sliders, as though the trolleybuses were 'fumista' trams in Portugal – only the climate of Walsall was wrong! *R. T. Wilson*

Above It was the poet Thomas Hood who concluded a humorous poem with the awful pun,'They went and told the sexton and the sexton tolled the bell'. The signs that tolled the death knell of the joint trolleybus service between Walsall and Wolverhampton were those put up alongside Wolverhampton Road in Bentley on the way to Willenhall, warning of construction traffic from the M6 motorway crossing the route. An agreement had been reached with Wolverhampton Corporation that the joint service should remain intact until 1967, irrespective of what happened to the rest of the dwindling green-and-yellow-liveried trolleybuses. Unfortunately, the line of the motorway cut right across the 29 trolleybus route, and after struggling with the construction traffic for several months, the inevitable closure was bowed to on 31 October 1965.

In late 1962 Walsall Corporation 351 (ADX 189), a former Ipswich vehicle with the destination aperture showing the strange diagonal 29 service lettering, has just negotiated the temporary traffic lights on its way towards Willenhall. Travelling towards the M6 road works and, in some ways, oblivion, is Wolverhampton's 638 (FJW 638). This Guy BT trolleybus had a very similar Park Royal body to that of 351. *D. R. Harvey collection*

Left Coming from Walsall into the centre of Willenhall, with Walsall Street behind it, is 339 (NDH 956) working on the 29 service. This was one of the ten Walsall Brush H30/26R-bodied Sunbeam F4s fitted with BTH 209D 95hp motors. It has been repainted in the all-over blue livery but is still well presented even to the extent of having black-painted front wings, although in actual fact they look more like rubber ones. It is travelling round the island at the Royal George, which in the early 1960s was an Atkinson's house. Atkinson's Aston Park Brewery was bought by Mitchells & Butlers in 1959, but under the terms of the take-over the pub signs had to remain for another ten years. Behind the trolleybus is a Walsall-registered Austin A55 van, followed by a Skoda 'Octavia' two-door saloon, both vehicles dating from about 1961. *R. F. Mack*

Above One of Wolverhampton's Guy BT trolleybuses negotiates the same island in the middle of Willenhall in the mid-1950s. The driver looks anxiously in his cab mirror to glimpse his conductress, money bag over her shoulder but sans ticket machine, running across the exit from Bilston Street to pull the frog back for the next passing trolleybus. In the distance in Walsall Street, a Bedford 'O' series lorry is about to pass the site of Willenhall Library. The only visible cars, parked on the right, are a Jowett 10hp four-door saloon of about 1938 and a Ford Ten Model 7W of about the same year. The trolleybus will park on the hard standing behind the photographer. *C. W. Routh*

Below A third-hand Leyland National 10351A/2R of Chase Coaches, 57 (AYR 343T), which entered service in August 1979, comes into the centre of Willenhall past the Royal George working on Chase's 5 service to Bilston. Most of the old buildings from the days of the trolleybus have remained, and the pub, dating from 1847, has certainly been gentrified considerably in the more than 35 years since the previous views. One of the delights of Willenhall today is that although the nearby Market Place has been pedestrianised, many of the 19th-century buildings are well cared for and remain in everyday use. In a break between heavy spring showers, on Tuesday 6 April 1999, only the large traffic island at the bottom of Willenhall's Market Place appears to have gone, having been replaced by a much smaller, somewhat battle-scarred 'mini-island'. *D. R. Harvey*

Above One of the former Ipswich Corporation Park Royal-bodied Sunbeam F4s, 345 (ADX 194), turns back towards Walsall at the entrance to the Market Place in Willenhall. It is on a short working corresponding to the original Walsall trolleybus route of 1931. The trolleybus, later to be preserved by the Reading Trolleybus Society in Ipswich livery, has turned in front of the Midland Bank and the seated Wolverhampton *Express & Star* newspaper vendor and will pull up alongside the Royal George, before heading back by way of Walsall Street towards Townend Bank. *J. G. Simpson*

Below Echoing the days of electric tramcar services, Wolverhampton's 25 service from Willenhall to Bilston and Fighting Cocks started in Bilston Street and was physically linked to the Walsall to Wolverhampton service at Willenhall Market Place. What normally never happened was a Walsall trolleybus venturing on to the Bilston Street route – except for possible emergencies, and later when trolleybus tours were being organised. Wolverhampton Corporation 485 (FJW 485), a Guy BT with a Park Royal body of 1949, waits at the terminus with its poles down as Walsall's 870 (XDH 70) glides by on an enthusiasts' tour that will take the 30-foot-long F4A to such unlikely destinations as Bilston and Dudley. *D. R. Harvey collection*

Above Once beyond Willenhall the jointly operated trolleybus route ran under the wires of Wolverhampton Corporation. The trolleybuses went out of Willenhall by way of New Road and, on reaching the long, wide straight section of Willenhall Road, were able to 'stretch their legs'. Sunbeam W 308 (BDY 814), the former Hastings Tramways 39, had been purchased in 1959 after Maidstone & District closed down its subsidiary on 31 May 1959. Fitted with a Weymann H30/26R body, this vehicle, built in 1947, entered service on 19 August 1959, and is seen soon afterwards in Willenhall Road, passing the 1950s flats that had replaced the old, time-expired properties. *R. F. Mack*

Below The terminus in Walsall was in Horseley Fields opposite St James's Square, an area that has all but disappeared under the dual-carriageway Middle Cross Inner Ring Road section. In many ways the 29 route terminus was typical of trolleybus services throughout the country. The service was extremely efficient and covered an important route sector in this part of the Black Country, but both town termini were unimpressive and tucked out of sight. From beginning to end, right down to Porto, Portugal, the last place in the world to operate double-deck trolleybuses, whose town terminus was in Bolhao behind the city's main market, trolleybuses always seemed to 'lurk' in side streets. In about 1947 236 (JDH 433), a Roe 'relaxed' utility-bodied Sunbeam W that had entered service in February 1946, stands loading up its passengers before embarking on the return journey to Willenhall and Walsall. The conductor, having just finished his mug of tea, appears to be gathering his strength before 'ringing the driver off' and starting his job collecting the fares. *R. A. Mills*

Above The Wolverhampton short-working service to Willenhall was numbered 5 and reached the Market Place from Nechells on 19 September 1927. The green and yellow trolleybus, 489 (FJW 489), a 1949 Guy BT with a Park Royal H28/26R body, stands in Horseley Fields in October 1950, about to work to Willenhall. Behind it is Walsall trolleybus 231 (JDH 339), a utility Park Royal-bodied Sunbeam W that had entered service on 1 August 1945, and which will work all the way back to its home town. Ironically, this older, less well-equipped trolleybus would remain in service until July 1965, some two years after the newer trolleybus in front of it had been despatched to Don Everall for breaking up. The quite early advertisement for Wrigleys DK Spearmint chewing-gum – remember those little white sugar-coated squares of gum? – contrasts with the other beverages being advertised on the two trolleybuses. *A. B. Cross*

Below The St James's Square terminus in Wolverhampton had the advantage of being a wide open space at the town end of Horseley Fields, but had the disadvantage of being a little way outside Wolverhampton's town centre. Several ladies make their way towards the waiting trolleybus, although their chances of getting on it seem somewhat remote. Walsall's 323 (JDH 30) appears to be already full up with its quota of 56 passengers as it prepares to leave on another journey on the 29 service back to Walsall. It was one of the first wartime trolleybuses to be withdrawn, but in this late 1950s view its paintwork is positively gleaming. *D. Williams*

Above The Walsall Corporation trolleybus standing in the St James's Square trolleybus turning circle is 346 (ADX 195), the former Ipswich Corporation 125, a Sunbeam F4 with a Park Royal body built in 1950, entering service in March 1962. The turning loop had the advantage of allowing trolleybuses to 'stand down' and wait for the main-line trolleybuses to pass them, although it was perhaps surprising that there was no second running line on the overhead to allow for overtaking without the need to de-pole. The Wolverhampton vehicle is 409 (DJW 939), a wartime Sunbeam W chassis that had been rebodied in 1952 by Park Royal, and was withdrawn in 1965. It is working on the 5 turn-back service to Willenhall, while the former Ipswich trolleybus is going all the way through to Townend Bank. *D. Williams*

Above right On a bright sunny day the crew of the Walsall Corporation bus stand in front of their charge, 250 (MDH 335), a 1949 Guy 'Arab' III 5LW with a Park Royal H30/26R body. Despite being only about three years old, the composite bodywork around the lower saloon window edges is beginning to show signs of unevenness. It is parked at the Queen Street terminus on the 60 service through to Bloxwich by way of Wednesfield and New Invention. The through service was jointly operated by both Walsall and Wolverhampton Corporation and the route was divided at the Gate Inn, New Invention, with each Corporation being responsible for their section of the route on each side. The bleak nature of the buildings reveals just how run-down were the inner areas of many of Britain's towns in the early post-war period. Car traffic was nearly non-existent, with old cars having to soldier on until the mid-1950s, so bus services like this were always well subscribed. *M. Rooum*

Above Walsall Corporation Guy 'Arab' III 107 (MDH 317) turns out of Victoria Square in the centre of Wolverhampton when working on the 60 service in 1950. The year-old Park Royal-bodied bus leaves behind the hoardings surrounding the Square, which are advertising the current and forthcoming attractions at the Clifton and Olympia cinemas, the Repertory Theatre company production at the nearby Grand Theatre in Lichfield Street, the Ideal Home Exhibition at Birmingham's Bingley Hall, and a series of Bible Lectures every Sunday in London's Olympia. The only advertisements for products appear to be for Ansells beers, Oxo stock cubes and Gold Flake cigarettes. The area where the two cars are parked, one of which is a Morris Twelve, is where many of Wolverhampton's trolleybus services terminated. *A. B. Cross*

Below In January 1996 it was decided that certain West Midlands double-deckers would be repainted in the liveries of the former municipal fleets and would operate as part of a 'Heritage Fleet' of buses and represent the old Corporations in those towns. The bus chosen to be repainted in Walsall Corporation livery was 2888 (C888 FON), an MCW 'Metrobus' MkII DR102/48 with an MCW H43/30F body. It entered service originally in August 1985. All the former Corporation liveries, Birmingham, Coventry, Walsall, West Bromwich and Wolverhampton, looked infinitely better than the standard TWM livery. On 23 March 1999 2888 travels along Market Street in Wolverhampton when working on the 560 service. The beautifully replicated livery, even to the extent of the legal lettering being in the correct Corporation 'house style', is a fitting tribute to Walsall Corporation and has lasted extremely well, being by this time three years old. *D. R. Harvey*

A late entry into Birmingham

Sutton, Aldridge and Kingstanding

Services to the east of the town began in the 1920s and again created a situation that gave the Corporation very little opposition from Midland Red. The 53 service in the Streetly and Aldridge areas, jointly operated with West Bromwich Corporation, began as a single-deck route in October 1948, but by

1954 had been converted to double-deck operation.

It was perhaps a feeling that Walsall was something of a poor relation that led to the Sutton Coldfield terminus not being in The Parade, the town's main shopping street, but tucked away in Victoria Road. Even West Bromwich managed to get into the South Parade in 1947, but not Walsall. Today Victoria Road forms part of a ring road around the town centre, but during all of

Wet, steamed-up and miserable - and that was only the bus crew! Walsall Corporation ran its 6 service to the Royal Burgh of Sutton Coldfield, and together with West Bromwich Corporation was the only interloper into what was Midland Red territory. Until just before the Second World War double-deck operation had been forbidden in Sutton, much to the chagrin of Midland Red, which, having operated in the town since the earliest days of the company, was in dire need of extra seating capacity on its services.

Walsall's Corporation's first post-war order followed on from its successful wartime allocation and subsequent operation of Guy 'Arabs', except that these 1949-vintage

buses were the Mark III model. Fifty of these MDH-registered buses were ordered and all had Park Royal H30/26R bodies. Unlike their cousins in Wolverhampton, some of which, ordered about the same time, had similar Park Royal bodywork, the Walsall vehicles had standard crash-gearboxes and the small 7.0-litre Gardner 5LW engine. As the Walsall-specification bodies were lightweight to the point of being flimsy, perhaps their power-to-weight ratio was better than might have been expected. Here 99 (MDH 315) stands outside Victoria Road Junior School in company with a Ford Anglia 100E, which in hindsight looks vaguely like an East German Trabant P600 saloon. *R. F. Mack*

Walsall's days of operation it was little more than a side road.

The route to Sutton Coldfield did not run in competition with West Bromwich, but the latter's service 25, from Dartmouth Square, linked with Walsall's 58 service at Kingstanding Circle. It was not unusual to see a green and white bus of Harper Brothers, a two-tone blue vehicle of West Bromwich Corporation and an all-over blue one of Walsall just on a nodding acquaintance with the buses of Birmingham City Transport.

Above Walsall Corporation's 6 route in and out of Sutton Coldfield would have been worthy of a trolleybus route! Climbing up Coleshill Street in the early 1960s, with the much-rebuilt, Victorian-clad Holy Trinity Parish Church behind the wall on the right and a group of attractive Georgian brick houses on the left, is 182 (ODH 99). This was one of the full-front, Park Royal-bodied Guy 'Arab' IIIs, fitted this time with the more powerful Gardner 6LW 8.4-litre six-cylinder diesel engine. As it barks its way up the hill, passing another of the well-selling Ford Anglia 100Es, the double-decker will begin to make its way out of the town on its way towards Aldridge. *R. F. Mack*

Below On leaving Aldridge, the 6 service returned to Walsall by way of Walsall Road. This is now the A454 and, as well as the industrial works on the right behind the bus, has now got housing a good deal further along it, although the farmland at Berryfields Farm survives. Walsall's Daimler 'Fleetline' CRG6LW 10 (2740 DH) was one of the original production batch of 27ft 6in, short-length Northern Counties H44/29F buses, delivered in February 1964. With their driving position over the front axle, they were very pleasant to ride in as they 'held the road' extremely well. Unfortunately, with their centre entrance and sliding door, they were not designed for One-man-Operation. After acquisition by WMPTE, nearly all were converted to a dual-door layout, which placed a single-leaf door opposite the driver. This conversion was undertaken by Lex Garages of Stourbridge, and while successful was aesthetically quite awful. The job was turned down by the original body-builder, Northern Counties, and Willowbrook, who also tendered, failed to win the contract. The bus is speeding past Longwood Lane on its way back to Walsall by way of Mellish Road and the Arboretum. It is followed by a Ford Consul 204E of the sort that had a 'lowline' roof, in production from February 1959 until 1962. *D. R. Harvey collection*

Above A large number of Walsall's 'bread and butter' services were around the many council estates that grew up in the years before and after the Second World War. At that time the policy was not for the introduction of new trolleybus services – that would come after Edgley Cox and the Blakenall extension of 1955. The result was that many of the outlying areas were always going to be operated by motor buses. Here Guy 'Arab' III 5LW 112 (MDH 321), a Park Royal-bodied double-decker of 1949, works through such a housing area on the 12 service, which operated from here in Bloxwich back to Walsall, but by way of Pelsall and Rushall. *R. F. Mack*

Below For many years, until the spring of 1965, Walsall Corporation reached only as far as the notice-boards that marked the Birmingham City boundary and no further! This was at The Circle, Kingstanding, when their buses were working on the 50 or 58 services from Bloxwich or Aldridge. With a BCT Crossley-bodied Daimler CVG6 on the other side of the large traffic island working on the 29A route, which itself terminated in Aldridge (but only just!), Walsall Corporation's 802 (PDH 802) waits in Kingstanding Road, outside the operational area of the Corporation. It is working on the 50 route, which will take it back to Bloxwich by way of Aldridge and Pelsall. The single-decker is a Leyland 'Royal Tiger' PSU1/13 and had Leyland's own attractive B44F body, characterised by its shallow roof-line. *D. Williams*

The 58 service also terminated at The Circle, Kingstanding, having arrived by way of Pelsall and Shelfield. On 26 June 1963 the first prototype Crossley 'Bridgemaster', 825 (YDH 225), stands in Kingstanding Road with the mock-Jacobean Kingstanding public house, dating from the early 1930s, in the background. This attractive, though far too large, hostelry was demolished after barely 40 years of use and replaced by a shopping centre and a much smaller, more anonymous pub. Kingstanding was named after a minor incident in 1642 when, according to local legend, King Charles I reviewed his troops here at the beginning of the Civil War before the Battle of Edge Hill. The whole area was developed by Birmingham Corporation in the 1920s, when one of the largest municipal housing developments in Europe was built here. With Walsall's 825 reaching this close to Birmingham, one wonders if it ever 'crossed tyres' with its identical twin, the second 'Bridgemaster', the former ACV demonstrator 9 JML, which became BCT's 3228. *W. Ryan*

Birmingham at last!

On 21 June 1965 Walsall Corporation successfully applied to the West Midlands Traffic Commissioners, with Harper Brothers of Heath Hayes, to extend its Aldridge to Kingstanding route into Birmingham city centre to terminate in Union Street. This was granted only because BCT had not vigorously defended its territory, as it usually did, and by the time the General Manager, Mr Copestake, had returned from a vacation the 'damage', or the 'prize', depending upon which side of the fence one sat, was done or won. Walsall was in! The route was numbered 158 and, to add insult to injury, there was also an express service covering the same route to Bloxwich, numbered 958.

Within a short period of time Walsall was in again, this time taking over some of the running on the 118 Midland Red service through Perry Barr, along Walsall Road and out to Great Barr. This had been the notion of the Corporation in its Edwardian tram days, so for its last three full years of operation Walsall had extended its operation into Birmingham on two routes and in neither case was working with BCT.

Above right The Birmingham Road tram service had been served by the Corporation since 1 January 1904 and was the second one to close on 29 September 1928. Walsall had obtained powers under the Walsall Corporation Act of 1900 to operate trams beyond the boundary at the Bell Inn, across the 'no man's land' of Great Barr to the Scott Arms. There were even proposals to extend the service along Walsall Road to meet up with the Birmingham number 6 tram service, which terminated just under 3 miles from the Bell

Inn near Perry Barr railway station outside the New Crown and Cushion. Unfortunately the intervening local authorities would not authorise these proposals and what might have been a most interesting inter-urban tram route was still-born. Car 14, one of the original 1904 open-topped Brush-built cars, accelerates out of Ablewell Street into Birmingham Road in about 1908, before Springhill Road was built. The five young boys, one barefoot and another apparently eating from a bag, watch as the photographer captures the moment. *Walsall Local Studies Library*

Above Travelling out of Walsall is tramcar 27, one of the Brush open-toppers that was still in its original condition. It has just passed the Six Ways junction, with Sutton Road to the left of the attractively foliaged grounds of the early-19th-century house. This area of Walsall had only begun to be seriously developed in the last few years of the 1890s, and just out of sight the land was largely still used for farming. The tram will begin the gentle descent towards the old Malt Shovel public house. The Birmingham Road route was the shortest of all Walsall's tram routes and, when opened, terminated at the Walsall boundary well into the open countryside. Its main traffic in the summer would have been passengers travelling to the high land that afforded good views over Birmingham and the surrounding areas. Without the possibility of a further tramway extension, the Birmingham Road tram route was inevitably going to be an early candidate for conversion to buses. *D. R. Harvey collection*

Top The elegantly dressed woman, in her long white dress, stands in front of the newest of the Edwardian houses in Birmingham Road on a sunny day in about 1908. The distant tram, Car 16, one of the six fitted with Milnes-Voss Balloon-roofed enclosed top-decks, stands further down the hill on the single track line in Birmingham Road. At this time the tram still retains its open platforms, which will not be vestibuled until during the First World War. Within a few years this track would be doubled, thus allowing for a much improved service frequency. The tramcar, the only form of mechanised transport in Birmingham Road, is near the junction with Jesson Road. *Commercial postcard*

Middle Standing at the Bell Inn terminus of the 26 service is a much altered bus. It is 13 (JDH 104), a 1944 Guy 'Arab' II 5LW that originally had a Park Royal wartime H30/26R body. The condition of these wooden bodies deteriorated so much that Walsall Corporation embarked upon an extensive rebodying programme of the robust Guys between 1950 and 1952, using pre-war Park Royal bodies from time-expired Dennis 'Lance' chassis. In this case 13 received the body from the former 118 (DDH 150), which in its prime had been the first of the 1936 batch of 'Lances'. In this condition 13 would manage another 12 years in service. Behind the Guy is an almost new MCCW-bodied BMMO D7, working on the 118 service from Birmingham via the Scott Arms. *7 Valley Productions*

Bottom After finally getting into Birmingham in 1965 via Kingstanding with the joint service with Harper Brothers of Heath Hayes, it was not long before a similar agreement was entered into with Midland Red. This enabled the original Edwardian tramway plans to be realised as the jointly operated 118 service went from Walsall to the Bell Inn and on to Great Barr, Perry Barr and Birmingham via Six Ways, Aston. Waiting at the Scott Arms near Newton Road is 896 (896 MDH), a 30-foot-long AEC 'Regent' V 2D2RA with a Willowbrook H41/31F body, which had entered service in August 1961, and is working on the 118 route to Walsall. This important route was the only one of the insurgents that offered a service into the centre of Walsall, as the 158 route went to Bloxwich. The Scott Arms was built in the 1870s, but demolished in May 1966 and replaced by a shopping centre and an anonymous new pub. *D. Williams*

Above As we have seen, Mr Ronald Edgley Cox could not be accused of being orthodox in his ordering policy. In the spring of 1968 he ordered the only Daimler 'Fleetline' CRC6-36 to be delivered for to the British market. The Cummins V6-200-engined chassis had been developed for Johannesburg Municipal Transport, but this one was sent for bodying to Northern Counties, which was still building short-length 'Fleetlines' for Walsall; Northern Counties must have thought that they had gone from 'the sublime to the gor blimey'! The engine was mounted longitudinally in the chassis frame, so as well as a front entrance, a rear entrance was also specified together with two staircases. With a seating capacity of 86, of which 51 were on the top deck, the rear staircase was viewed in the cab of this intended One-Man-Operated bus by a television monitor! The bus was exhibited at the 1968 Commercial Motor Show and entered service as 56, (XDH 56G), but was never operated as a one-man vehicle, no doubt much to the delight of the drivers. It was to lead a lonely, unloved existence both with Walsall and, within a year, West Midlands PTE and it is in the latter's ownership that it is seen in New Street working on the 118 service to St Paul's Bus Station, Walsall, in company with an ex-BCT 'Fleetline' 3274, (274 GON). *L. Mason*

Right Birmingham at last! The city centre terminus of the 158 service was at the Corporation Street end of Union Street, alongside the then derelict City Arcade. Union Street had replaced Martineau Street on 16 October 1960 as the city terminus for a number of Birmingham bus services, including the 33 service to Kingstanding, so for reasons of continuity it was used for the Walsall Corporation/Harper Brothers service, which began on 21 June 1965. Walsall's 98 (RDH 98F0, a short-length Daimler 'Fleetline' CRG6LX with a Northern Counties H41/29D body – how did they get so many in? – stands outside the closed-down shops by the City Arcade in Union Street in early 1969. The driver and conductor are doing what every driver and conductor have done throughout this volume – standing, in this case on the platform of the bus, and having a good natter, although experience suggests that it was more likely to be a moan! *L. Mason*

Walsall Corporation services

All services originated in 1935 except those marked with an asterisk (*), which date from 1965. Those in **bold** are trolleybus routes, while those in *italics* are schools or works services.

1	WALSALL-CANNOCK-HEDNESFORD
2	BLOXWICH-NEW INVENTION-WILLENHALL
3	WALSALL-FULLBROOK
4	WALSALL-PELSALL-BROWNHILLS-HEATH HAYES
5	WALSALL-CHASETOWN-HEDNESFORD
6	WALSALL-ALDRIDGE-SUTTON COLDFIELD
7	HEDNESFORD-PYE GREEN-CANNOCK
8	CANNOCK-HEDNESFORD-RAWNSLEY
9	WALSALL-WALSALL WOOD-SHENSTONE
10	WALSALL-REEDSWOOD
11	WALSALL-PELSALL-BROWNHILLS-RISING SUN INN
12	WALSALL-PELSALL-BLOXWICH
13	WALSALL-STREETLY
14	WALSALL-FULLBROOK-STONE CROSS-WEST BROMWICH (joint with West Bromwich)
15	**WALSALL-BLAKENALL-BLOXWICH-LEAMORE-WALSALL** (Circular)
16	WALSALL-WALSALL WOOD-MUCKLEY CORNER-LICHFIELD
17	WALSALL-NORTON-HEATH HAYES-CANNOCK-CHESLYN HAY
18	BLOXWICH-CHESLYN HAY-GREAT WYRLEY
19	WALSALL-BROWNHILLS-CHASETOWN-BURNTWOOD
20	CANNOCK-RUGELEY via OLD HEDNESFORD ROAD
20*	WALSALL-PRIMLEY AVENUE
21	WALSALL-BARR COMMON-BLOXWICH
21*	WALSALL-RUSHALL-ALDRIDGE
21*	WALSALL-DELVES HOTEL
22	HEATH HAYES-CANNOCK-CHESLYN HAY
22*	WALSALL-WALSTEAD ROAD-YEW TREE ESTATE
23	WALSALL-WALSALL WOOD-BROWNHILLS STATION-OGLEY HAY-WALSALL WOOD-WALSALL
24	WALSALL-PADDOCK-WALSALL
25	WALSALL-PLECK ROAD
25*	BLOXWICH-ESSINGTON-NEW INVENTION
26	WALSALL-BIRMINGHAM ROAD (MERRIONS CLOSE)
27	HEDNESFORD-HAZEL SLADE-CANNOCK WOOD-BEAUDESERT
28	WALSALL-WILLENHALL
28*	RUGELEY-PEAR TREE FARM ESTATE
29	**WALSALL-WILLENHALL-WOLVERHAMPTON** (joint with Wolverhampton)
30	**WALSALL-LEAMORE-BLOXWICH-BLAKENALL-WALSALL** (Circular)
31	BLOXWICH-NEW INVENTION
31*	**WALSALL-LEAMORE-BLOXWICH-MOSSLEY ESTATE**
32	BRADFORD PLACE-WALSTEAD ROAD-DELVES
32*	**WALSALL-LEAMORE-BLOXWICH-LOWER FARM ESTATE**
33	CANNOCK-WIMBLEBURY-HEDNESFORD
33*	**WALSALL-LEAMORE-BLOXWICH-CAVENDISH ROAD-BEECHDALE ESTATE**
34	WALSALL-LEAMORE
34*	WESTGATE-RUSHALL-WALSALL-BESCOT-DELVES
35.	WALSALL-PLECK-INNER CIRCLE-PLECK
36	WALSALL-WALSALL WOOD-CANNOCK-HEDNESFORD via HUNTINGTON TERRACE
36*	WALSALL-WALSALL WOOD (CASTELFORT ESTATE)
37	WALSALL-PLECK-WEDNESBURY-DARLASTON-PLECK-WALSALL (Circular)
38	WALSALL-PLECK-DARLASTON-WEDNESBURY-PLECK-WALSALL (Circular)
39	WALSALL-PLECK
39*	CANNOCK-LIME PIT LANE-CANNOCK (Circular, joint with Midland Red)
40	WILLENHALL-WOOD LANE ESTATE
41	WALSALL-NEW INVENTION-WILLENHALL
42	CANNOCK-BELT ROAD via BLACKFORDS
42*	BLOXWICH-BEECHDALE ESTATE
43	CHASE TERRACE-BEAUDESERT
44	BONEY HAY-CHASE TERRACE-LICHFIELD
45	BEAUDESERT-BURNTWOOD-HAMMERWICH-LICHFIELD
46	GOOSEMOOR GREEN-BURNTWOOD-LICHFIELD
47*	LICHFIELD-BURNTWOOD-HEATH HAYES-CANNOCK
48*	WALSALL-RUSHALL-HIGH HEATH-SHELFIELD
49*	WALSALL-GOSCOTE-BLAKENHALL-BLOXWICH
50*	BLOXWICH-PELSALL-SHELFIELD-ALDRIDGE-KINGSTANDING
51*	BENTLEY-DARLASTON-WEDNESBURY
52*	CANNOCK-LONGFORD ROAD-CANNOCK (Circular)
53*	STREETLY-ALDRIDGE-SCOTT ARMS-WEST BROMWICH (joint with West Bromwich)
54*	WALSALL-YEW TREE ESTATE -STONE CROSS-WEST BROMWICH (joint with West Bromwich)
55*	WALSALL-RUSHALL-ALDRIDGE-KINGSTANDING

56* WALSALL-RUSHALL-ALDRIDGE
57* ALDRIDGE-WHITE HOUSE INN-ALDRIDGE
(Circular, joint with West Bromwich)
58* BLOXWICH-PELSALL-SHELFIELD-WESTGATE-
KINGSTANDING
59* WALSALL-ALDRIDGE (joint with West Bromwich)
60* BLOXWICH-NEW INVENTION-WEDNESFIELD-
WOLVERHAMPTON (joint with Wolverhampton)
61* HEDNESFORD-LITTLEWORTH-HAZEL SLADE
62* BROWNHILLS-HAMMERWICH-LICHFIELD
63* BLOXWICH-ESSINGTON-SHARESHILL
65* DUDLEY-TIPTON-WEDNESBURY-PLECK-
WALSALL-BLOXWICH-CANNOCK-STAFFORD
(joint with Midland Red 865)
66* HEDNESFORD-HEATH HAYES
69* WALSALL-BROWNHILLS-BURNTWOOD
HOSPITAL
73* WALSALL-PRINCES AVENUE-SUTTON ROAD-
BARR BEACON-STREETLY
74* WALSALL-THE CRESCENT-SUTTON ROAD-
BARR BEACON-STREETLY
75* WALSALL-BARR BEACON-STREETLY-
BARR BEACON-NEW OSCOTT-BARR BEACON-
WALSALL (Circular, joint with Midland Red 115)
76* WALSALL-THE CRESCENT-SUTTON ROAD-
BARR BEACON-BRIDLE LANE-STREETLY
77* WALSALL-BARR BEACON-NEW OSCOTT-
SUTTON COLDFIELD-STREETLY-
BARR BEACON-WALSALL (Circular, joint with
Midland Red 117)
101* WALSALL (BRADFORD PLACE)-
DARLASTON GREEN
102* WALSALL (TOWNEND BANK)-
DARLASTON GREEN
103* *WALSALL-BLOXWICH-
MID-CANNOCK COLLIERY-CANNOCK*
104* *WALSALL (CALTHORPE ROAD)-
CHUCKERY SCHOOLS*
105* *WALSALL-ALDRIDGE-STREETLY WORKS*
106* *WALSALL-BARR BEACON-STREETLY WORKS*
107* *KINGSTANDING (ODEON)-RED HOUSE
INDUSTRIAL ESTATE*
108* *HEDNESFORD-LITTLETON COLLIERY*
109* *CANNOCK-HEDNESFORD-BRINDLEY HEATH
COLLIERY*
111* *BENTLEY-DARLASTON GRAMMAR SCHOOL*
115* *WALSALL-BLOXWICH-WYRLEY No3
COLLIERY*

116* *LONGFORD ROAD ESTATE, CANNOCK-
BRIDGTOWN SCHOOL, CANNOCK*
117* *MOSSLEY ESTATE-ELMORE GREEN INFANT
SCHOOL*
118* *WALSALL-PELSALL-BROWNHILLS-
WYRLEY No3 COLLIERY*
118* *WALSALL-SCOTT ARMS-BIRMINGHAM (NEW
STREET) (joint with Midland Red)*
120* *WALSALL-CHASETOWN-BURNTWOOD-
RAWNSLEY-BRINDLEY HEATH COLLIERY*
122* *WILLENHALL-NEW INVENTION-
ESSINGTON-HILTON MAIN COLLIERY*
123* *RUSHALL-BLOXWICH-
LITTLETON COLLIERY*
124* *CHASE TERRACE-BROWNHILLS-
WALSALL WOOD-CHUCKERY (CRABTREE
WORKS)*
132* *STREETLY WORKS-BRIDLE LANE-ALDRIDGE
(TYNING LANE)*
133* *MALT SHOVEL INN-DELVES-
WHITEHALL SCHOOL*
134* *BLOXWICH-PELSALL-
BROWNHILLS FACTORY ESTATE*
149* *LOWER FARM ESTATE-
GREEN ROCK ESTATE-BLAKENALL*
152* *LONGFORD ROAD ESTATE, CANNOCK-
WALSALL ROAD/GIRTON ROAD, CANNOCK*
158* BLOXWICH-PELSALL-SHELFIELD-WESTGATE-
ALDRIDGE-KINGSTANDING-PERRY BARR-
BIRMINGHAM (UNION STREET)
224* *BROWNHILLS-PELSALL-CHUCKERY
(CRABTREE WORKS)*
265* DUDLEY-TIPTON-WEDNESBURY-PLECK-
WALSALL (Midland Red)
324* *MOSSLEY-BLOXWICH-LEAMORE-CHUCKERY
(CRABTREE WORKS)*
333* *COALPOOL-BEECHDALE ESTATE*
424* *HEATH HAYES- NORTON-PELSALL-
CHUCKERY (CRABTREE WORKS)*
901 WALSALL-CANNOCK-HEDNESFORD (Limited-
stop)
958* BLOXWICH-PELSALL-RUSHALL-ALDRIDGE-
KINGSTANDING-PERRY BARR-BIRMINGHAM
(UNION STREET) (Limited-stop)
960* LICHFIELD-MUCKLEY CORNER-
BROWNHILLS-PELSALL-BLOXWICH-
WOLVERHAMPTON (Limited-stop)

Walsall Corporation tram tickets, reproduced actual size

Tram and bus drawings

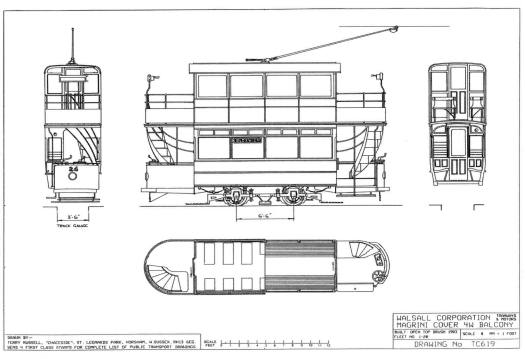

DRAWN BY:-
TERRY RUSSELL, "CHACESIDE", ST. LEONARDS PARK, HORSHAM, W.SUSSEX, RH13 6EG.
SEND 4 FIRST CLASS STAMPS FOR COMPLETE LIST OF PUBLIC TRANSPORT DRAWINGS.

SCALE
FEET 0 1 2 3 4 5 6 7 8 9 10 11 12

WALSALL CORPORATION TRAMWAYS & MOTORS
MAGRINI COVER 4W BALCONY
BUILT: OPEN TOP BRUSH 1903   SCALE 4 MM = 1 FOOT
FLEET No. 1-28
DRAWING No TC619

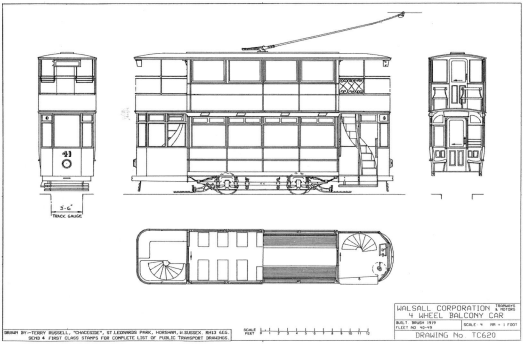

DRAWN BY:-TERRY RUSSELL, "CHACESIDE", ST.LEONARDS PARK, HORSHAM, W.SUSSEX, RH13 6EG.
SEND 4 FIRST CLASS STAMPS FOR COMPLETE LIST OF PUBLIC TRANSPORT DRAWINGS.

SCALE
FEET 0 1 2 3 4 5 6 7 8 9 10 11 12

WALSALL CORPORATION TRAMWAYS & MOTORS
4 WHEEL BALCONY CAR
BUILT: BRUSH 1919   SCALE 4 MM = 1 FOOT
FLEET No. 40-49
DRAWING No TC620

Opposite left 1-28 class Brush open-topper rebuilt with a Magrini top-cover. *Terry Russell*

Opposite below left 40-49 class Brush vestibuled, open-balcony car. *Terry Russell*

A nearside drawing of one of the full-front-bodied Guy 'Arab' III 6LWs of 1951.

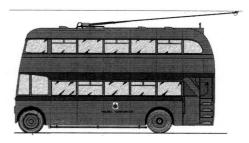

One of the ten Sunbeam F4s with Brush H30/26R bodies. These were Walsall's first postwar trolleybuses and were delivered in 1951.

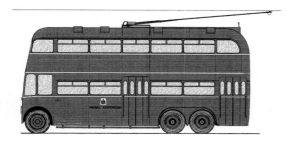

Walsall's only postwar six-wheeler: a Sunbeam S7 with a Willowbrook body in its original two-door condition. It was designed with two doors for Pay As You Board experiments.

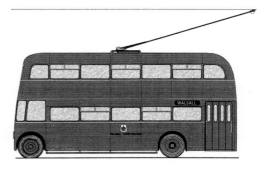

A 'Goldfish Bowl': a 30-foot-long Sunbeam F4A with a Willowbrook body that revolutionised the trolleybus system in Walsall.

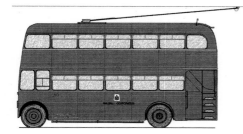

One of the ex-Grimsby-Cleethorpes BUT 9611Ts with Northern Coach Builders bodies that looked very similar to products built by Eastern Coach Works in Lowestoft. It is shown in its original condition.

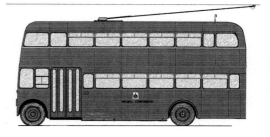

In pantomimes such as *Cinderella* there was always a transformation scene. Trolleybus 875 was similar in that it is shown here in its transformed 30-foot-long front-entrance state – a dramatic change from its original 56-seat rear-entrance condition.

Index of locations

Tailpiece: The evening of Sunday 31 October 1965 was very wet and distinctly miserable. It was also the last night of the jointly worked 29 trolleybus service between Walsall and Wolverhampton, the route's premature closure necessitated by the construction of the M6 motorway at Bentley. However, the service had been under threat anyway, as Wolverhampton was well on the way to abandoning its trolleybus system.

Later that night, while a small band of enthusiasts gathered to see off the last trolleybuses, the very last one from Wolverhampton, Walsall Corporation's 353 (ADX 191), one of the former Ipswich Corporation Sunbeam F4s, met the last trolleybus from Walsall. The latter was Wolverhampton's 434 (EJW 434), a Sunbeam W4 of 1947, which had been the town's first postwar trolleybus. It had been rebodied with a new Roe H32/28R body in 1960, but failed by a few months to last out until the final closure. The trolleybuses are passing at the operational half-way point on the route, in New Road at the Market Place, Willenhall, with the Atkinsons sign of the Royal George pub just visible beyond 353. *J. C. Brown*